KIDS!
PICTURE YOURSELF
Cooking

maranGraphics Inc.

Course Technology PTR
A part of Cengage Learning

 COURSE TECHNOLOGY
CENGAGE Learning™

Australia • Brazil • Japan • Korea • Mexico • Singapore • Spain • United Kingdom • United States

COURSE TECHNOLOGY
CENGAGE Learning

Kids! Picture Yourself Cooking

maranGraphics Inc.

Publisher and General Manager,
Course Technology PTR:
Stacy L. Hiquet

Associate Director of Marketing:
Sarah Panella

Manager of Editorial Services:
Heather Talbot

Marketing Manager: Jordan Casey

Acquisitions Editor: Megan Belanger

Content Editor: Q.L. Pearce

Project Editor: Sandy Doell

Technical Reviewer: Michelle Stern

Kid Reviewer: Shelby Hiquet

PTR Editorial Services Coordinator:
Erin Johnson

Interior Layout: Jill Flores

Cover Designer: Mike Tanamachi

Indexer: Katherine Stimson

Proofreader: Heather Urschel

For product information and technology assistance, contact us at
Cengage Learning Customer & Sales Support, 1-800-354-9706

For permission to use material from this text or product,
submit all requests online at **cengage.com/permissions**

Further permissions questions can be emailed to
permissionrequest@cengage.com

All trademarks are the property of their respective owners.

Library of Congress Control Number: 2008902395

ISBN-13: 978-1-59863-258-6

ISBN-10: 1-59863-258-5

Course Technology
25 Thomson Place
Boston, MA 02210
USA

Cengage Learning is a leading provider of customized learning solutions with office locations around the globe, including Singapore, the United Kingdom, Australia, Mexico, Brazil, and Japan. Locate your local office at: **international.cengage.com/region**

Cengage Learning products are represented in Canada by Nelson Education, Ltd.

For your lifelong learning solutions, visit **courseptr.com**

Visit our corporate website at **cengage.com**

Printed in the United States of America
1 2 3 4 5 6 7 11 10 09

Contents

Recipes

Introduction

Can you picture yourself cooking? For the new chef, the kitchen may seem a little scary. Don't worry. Even the world's greatest chefs had to start at the beginning. They had to learn simple tasks, such as how to boil water safely, crack open an egg, or measure ingredients.

In this book you will learn all of these skills. You will also find out about kitchen tools and common ingredients. By following the pictures, you will discover how to choose the right knife or pot for the job. You will get the hang of how to choose, prepare, use, and store ingredients. Before long you will be able to read a recipe like a pro, dice onions for a tasty beef stew, and stir up a batch of whipped cream for a yummy lemon pound cake. There are plenty of recipes included for you to try, so let's cook up some fun!

Safety in the Kitchen

Cooking is fun for the whole family. Always cook with an adult buddy, particularly when you are trying a new skill. Even though a chef handles sharp knives and hot pots and pans, cooking is safe as long as you follow a few guidelines.

Dress for Success

- Always wear an apron. It will protect you from spills.

- Do not wear baggy clothes, particularly baggy sleeves, when cooking. Loose clothing is a fire danger.

- Protect your feet. Barefoot is fun, but shoes protect your feet from dropped knives and hot spills.

- If you have long hair, tie it back away from your face.

Handling Heat

- When you are cooking, pay attention to what you are working on. Do not try to watch television or chat on the phone.

- When using a stove, turn pot handles toward the back so that they will not be knocked over by accident.

- Do not leave pots or pans unattended on high heat. Food can burn quickly and become a fire hazard. If food is on low heat, use a timer as a reminder to check it.

- Never taste or dip your fingers in hot food or lick hot utensils.

- Use only microwave-safe dishes and cookware in the microwave. Never put metal objects, cans, or aluminum foil in the microwave.

That's Sharp!

- Always handle knives with care. Be sure your hands are clean and dry when using a knife.

- Always keep your fingers curled away from the blade when you are using a knife.

- Do not put knives in soapy water in the sink because you might cut yourself by accident. Load knives in the dishwasher point down.

- If you must walk with a knife, carry it point down with the blade facing behind you.

- Remember that peelers, graters, blenders, and zesters are sharp, too. Handle them with care. Keep fingers and utensils away from the beaters of hand mixers or stand mixers.

Clean Up Time

- A clean kitchen is a safer kitchen. Don't stack pots, pans, or containers where they might fall.

- When you are finished cooking, wipe up spills, be sure appliances are off, and clean and put away dishes and utensils.

In an Emergency

- Always cook with an adult buddy. With an adult, review safety procedures in case of fire or injury.

- Know where to find the household first aid kit and fire extinguisher.

- In case of fire, never put water on the flames. That can spread them. If there is a small fire in a pan, let your adult buddy throw baking soda on it or cover it with a lid.

> **Tip** ● **Tip** ● **Tip** ● **Tip**
>
> Some people are allergic to wheat, nuts, fish, and other ingredients. Before you serve a dish that you have prepared, ask if anyone has any allergies and let them know if the food contains anything they are allergic to.
>
> **Tip** ● **Tip** ● **Tip** ● **Tip**

Handling Food Safely

No matter how clean you keep your kitchen, it is sure to have unwanted guests. Those are the germs, or bacteria, that can make you sick. Sometimes bacteria may stow away on food. Some may arrive with a friend or a pet. You cannot eliminate bacteria from your kitchen completely, but there are four simple guidelines to keep your food safe.

Clean

- Always wash your hands with hot soapy water before preparing food. Wash them again after handling raw meat, poultry, seafood, or raw eggs.

- Don't rush when it comes to hand washing. Sing a song such as "Happy Birthday" as you scrub. Don't stop until you have finished the song.

- Before you start to cook, wipe down your kitchen countertop with a damp fabric washcloth or a fresh paper towel. To dampen the cloth or paper towel, dip it in hot soapy water and wring it out.

- Wipe down or clean your cutting board, knives, and utensils before you use them.

- Always wash fruit and vegetables before you use them. Even if you plan to peel food, a knife cutting through peel can contaminate the fruit or vegetable underneath.

Separate

- Use a separate cutting board for preparing raw meat, poultry, and seafood.

- Store raw meat, poultry, and seafood in containers on the bottom shelf of the refrigerator until you are ready to use them. That prevents meat juices from dripping onto any other foods.

- Wash utensils after they have come in contact with raw eggs.

- Do not taste food you are cooking with a spoon or fork then put the utensil back into the food.

Cook

- Do not rinse raw meat or poultry. Rinsing can spread bacteria to your sink and counter-top. Cooking is the only way to kill bacteria.

- Cooking meat and poultry to the proper temperature will kill bacteria. Use a meat thermometer to be sure that the center of the meat is hot enough. Insert the thermometer into the center of the meat away from any bones. Wait at least 30 seconds before reading the temperature.

- Beef and pork should reach no less than 160°F. Ground poultry must reach 165°F. Poultry breasts should reach 170°F, and whole poultry should reach 180°F.

- Never taste anything with raw egg in it. That includes cookie dough.

Chill

- Do not overstuff your refrigerator. Cold air needs to circulate around food to keep it at the right temperature.

- Thaw foods in the refrigerator, not on the kitchen counter. It may take longer, but it is safer. Do not refreeze frozen foods that have become partially thawed.

- Do not put hot food directly into the freezer. It can cause other foods to thaw. Allow hot foods to cool slightly; then refrigerate them before putting them in the freezer.

- Refrigerate leftovers within 2 hours of cooking.

- Check expiration dates on packaged food to be sure it is fresh.

How to Use This Book

Kids! Picture Yourself Cooking is divided into two main sections. The first will introduce you to skills and ingredients that you will use in the kitchen. The second section includes a variety of recipes from starters to desserts. Begin by reviewing the Table of Contents. Be sure to read the guidelines for safety in the kitchen and for handling food safely.

Each topic or recipe page is highlighted with photographs that will help you to identify tools or ingredients, learn a skill or technique, or put together a delicious dish. You will also find special tips, charts, and fun facts that will help you to grow as a chef.

Each recipe includes a list of tools and ingredients you will need to make the dish. Read the recipe completely and gather the things you need before you start to cook.

You may come across cooking or preparation terms that you are not familiar with. You will find a glossary at the back of the book that defines many of these terms. There is also a Metric Conversion Chart if you find a recipe from another land that you would like to try.

Keep in mind that the recipes are a starting point. If you do not want to use a certain ingredient, or if you have an idea that might work better, give it a try. A good cook usually has a good imagination. The most important thing is to have fun and enjoy yourself in the kitchen.

Bon Appetit!

CHAPTER 1

To paint a picture, you need art brushes. To build a dog-house, you need a saw and a hammer. To do any job well, you need the right tools. Using the right tools in the kitchen can help you become a better cook.

Tools and Skills

Cutting Boards

Cutting boards may be made of wood, plastic, or disposable plastic. They offer a safe nonslip cutting surface, protect the counter, and make clean-up easier. If possible, use a different board for each type of food you cut. For example, use one for cutting vegetables and fruit, another for breads, and a third for raw meat.

Mixing Bowls

You will use mixing bowls for mixing, whisking, and combining ingredients. Mixing bowls may be large, small, and everything in between. They can be made of plastic or glass, but many cooks prefer stainless steel bowls because they are lightweight, sturdy, and easy to clean.

Colander and Strainer

When you are preparing a meal, you might have to drain some of your ingredients. A large, stainless steel colander is perfect for draining hot water from pasta. A medium-sized mesh strainer works great when you drain canned beans. If you need to strain the seeds from lemon or orange juice, try a small, fine mesh strainer.

Salad Spinner

When making a salad, it is important to wash lettuce, spinach, and other greens very carefully. A salad spinner is a handy tool that removes water from freshly washed leaves and herbs. This prevents limp, waterlogged greens from ruining your salad.

Vegetable Peeler

Vegetable peelers have a stainless steel double edge that removes the outer peel from fruits and vegetables such as cucumbers, apples, and potatoes. Peelers take a little getting used to, but with practice you can become an expert at removing a very thin layer of peel.

Liquid Measuring Cups

Liquid measuring cups come in a variety of sizes. The cups are marked with lines on the side that allow you to measure liquid ingredients such as milk or water. Clear glass measuring cups are the easiest to read. They are also the easiest to use when measuring hot ingredients such as boiling water or broth.

Dry Measuring Cups

Dry measuring cups are used with dry ingredients such as flour or sugar. They usually come in sizes with 1/4-cup, 1/3-cup, 1/2-cup, and 1-cup measures. Dry measuring cups are also handy for peanut butter, margarine, and other ingredients that are difficult to measure in a liquid measuring cup.

Measuring Spoons

Measuring spoons are ideal when you want to measure small amounts of spices, baking powder, oil, or vanilla. The spoons come in sets that include 1/8 teaspoon, 1/4 teaspoon, 1/2 teaspoon, 1 teaspoon, and 1 tablespoon.

Whisk

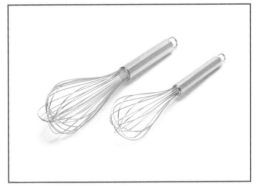

A whisk is good for whipping and beating by hand. Use a flexible balloon whisk for beating air into whipping cream. A narrow stiff whisk is best for eggs, sauces, and salad dressings.

Rubber Spatulas

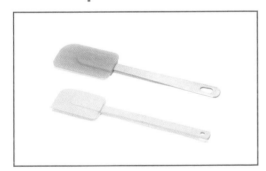

Used mainly for baking, flexible rubber spatulas scrape batter from mixing bowls. If you are stirring warm items such as custards, use a spatula made of heat-resistant nylon or heat- and stain-resistant silicone.

Pastry Brush

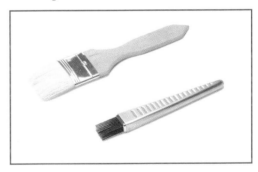

Whether you are baking or grilling, pastry brushes come in handy. They may be used to brush glazes onto breads, cakes, and fish, or to add seasoning to meats.

Meat Thermometer

A meat thermometer can take away the guess-work when you are roasting a chicken or baking a meatloaf. It will tell you the temperature deep inside the meat so that you will know when it has finished cooking.

Tongs

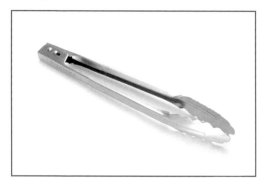

Tongs are useful for handling cooked foods such as pasta, meats, and vegetables. With tongs, you can move or lift food securely without piercing it.

Graters

The fastest way to grate a mound of cheese is to use a box grate. With different cutting edges on each side, this tool also allows you to slice or shred ingredients such as cheese, carrots, or potatoes into large coarse strips or fine thin strips. Small hand-held graters work well for ginger, fresh nutmeg, and chocolate.

FUN FACT

Cheese graters can sometimes be difficult to clean. If you are having a hard time removing sticky cheese from a box grater, run a piece of raw potato over the cutting edges. The potato will help to remove the cheese, and then you can wash the grater in hot, soapy water.

Spatula

When cooking eggs, pancakes, or hamburgers, you will have to turn the food over. A spatula is the perfect flipping tool. Lifting spatulas are usually flat with squared-off edges.

Potato Masher

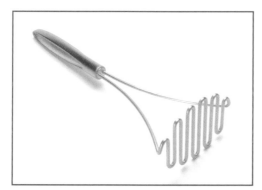

You might guess from its name that the main use of this tool is to mash cooked potatoes. It is handy for other jobs as well, such as mashing eggs for egg salad. A potato masher is usually made of stainless steel, with a wood or plastic handle.

FUN FACT

You can find specialized kitchen utensils in gourmet cooking stores. In addition to pizza cutters, you will find special knives just for cutting lettuce, special presses to make perfect hamburger patties, melon ballers, and hundreds of other gadgets to create all sorts of special effects.

Wooden Spoons

Wooden spoons are the best for stirring foods as they are cooking. The handles of the spoons don't get hot, and the wood won't harm cookware. You can find wooden spoons in many shapes and sizes.

Always look at a glass measuring cup from the side to make sure you've hit the correct mark. If you look from the top or from an angle to see if your liquid comes to the correct measurement, the liquid can distort your view.

Choosing a Knife

You should be able to grip the knife handle comfortably so that it doesn't slip. The knife should also feel balanced. That means that the handle and the blade should feel as if they weigh about the same.

Chef's Knife

A chef's knife is the most important knife in the kitchen. It can be used for many different cutting jobs, including mincing garlic, chopping vegetables, and carving meat.

A chef's knife is a large, weighty knife with a blade that is usually 8 to 10 inches long.

Knife Skills

When you are first learning to use a knife, ask a parent or adult helper to show you how to hold it. Watch as your helper cuts a few different types of foods. Ask your helper to watch you work with the knife. Start slowly. With a little practice, you can learn to handle your knife safely while preparing food with ease.

Hold the food that you are cutting firmly and always cut away from your body. After making a cut, move your hand holding the food to leave just enough space for the next cut. Be sure that the knife you are using is sharp. A dull blade can slip off of food unexpectedly.

If you have to walk with a knife in your hand, hold it at your side pointing downward. Be sure that the sharp edge is facing behind you. If you have to hand a knife to another person, set it down on the counter with the handle facing the other person.

The most common way to hold a knife is to grip the heel, or wide end, of the blade between your thumb and index finger. Wrap your other three fingers around the handle.

Bread Knife

A bread knife has a wavy, or serrated, blade. It can slice through bread or loaf cakes without crushing or tearing them.

A bread knife has a blade that is usually 8 to 10 inches long.

Paring Knife

A paring knife can be used for peeling and coring fruit and slicing mushrooms.

A paring knife is a small knife with a blade that is usually 2 to 4 inches long.

If you are cutting through something tough, place your thumb on the top of the blade. Wrap your other four fingers around the handle.

Hold food with your fingers curled slightly under and the tips of your fingers pointing back. This keeps them out of the way of the knife blade. Tuck your thumb safely behind your index finger.

As you make each cut, do not raise the sharp edge of the knife higher than the first knuckle of your fingers.

Make each cut slowly and carefully.

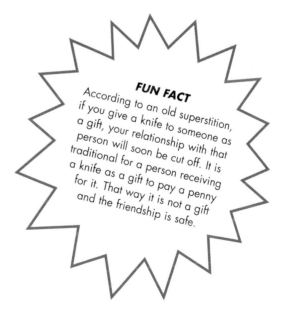

FUN FACT

According to an old superstition, if you give a knife to someone as a gift, your relationship with that person will soon be cut off. It is traditional for a person receiving a knife as a gift to pay a penny for it. That way it is not a gift and the friendship is safe.

Cookware

In the kitchen you will find a variety of pots and pans. Some are large. Some are small. They all have a special purpose, and most cooks have their favorites.

Choosing Cookware

Cookware is made of a variety of materials, each with distinct traits.

Stainless Steel

You can cook most kinds of food in stainless steel, but it may heat unevenly. Some cooks prefer stainless steel cookware with a copper-coated bottom to spread the heat.

Nonstick

Nonstick pans are easy to clean. They work well for most things, but not for jobs like glazing or caramelizing food.

Cast Iron

Cast iron is ideal for frying because it can take very high heat, but it is heavy. Cast iron skillets need a protective coating of oil and must be cleaned carefully without soap. Many cooks believe that the extra care is worth the effort. Some cast iron cookware comes coated with enamel.

Aluminum

These pots and pans distribute heat evenly, and they are usually lightweight. They are easy to clean but can become pitted over time. Anodized aluminum has a harder surface than regular aluminum.

Don't heat cookware with nothing in it. Over time, it can damage the cooking surface. Add oil or fluid and then heat. Add the food to be cooked once the pan is hot unless the recipe gives other instructions.

Use wooden, rubber, or plastic utensils if possible. They are less likely to scratch the surface.

Don't clean cookware with harsh scouring pads made of steel or iron. Use a sponge or a plastic scouring pad.

Stockpots and Dutch Ovens

A stockpot is a large, tall pot with a tight-fitting lid. This pot is used on a stovetop to cook soups and stews, and for boiling pasta. It should hold 8 quarts or more.

A Dutch oven is often used to cook soups, stews, and casseroles. It has a tight-fitting lid and is wider and shallower than a stockpot. It works well on a stovetop and can also fit in an oven if you are making a casserole. It should hold about 6 quarts.

Saucepans

Saucepans have long handles and tight-fitting lids. Large saucepans that hold 4 quarts or more are good for boiling potatoes and simmering rice. Small saucepans that hold 3 quarts or less are good for making sauces and boiling ingredients.

Skillets

A skillet may also be called a frying pan. With its long handle, wide surface, and low sides, a skillet is perfect for frying food. Skillets come in several sizes.

Sauté Pans

A sauté pan with a tight-fitting lid is good for browning meat, simmering chicken, or poaching fish. It has a long handle and straight or curved sides that are higher than the sides of a skillet.

Roasting Pans and Roasting Racks

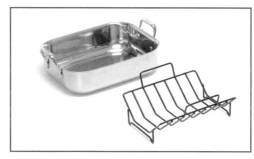

The job of the deep-sided roasting pan is roasting meat or baking lasagna. Most roasting pans are square and fit easily in an oven.

A roasting rack is a metal rack that fits into a roasting pan and keeps meat from touching the bottom of the pan. A roasting rack helps the meat to cook evenly and allows fat and juices to drain into the pan. The juices may be used later to make gravy.

Bakeware

If you want to bake cakes, cookies, or cupcakes, you will need to use bakeware. These pans and trays are made to fit into the oven and they will become very hot, so be sure to handle them carefully using hot pads or mitts.

Baking Sheets

Baking sheets are also called cookie sheets. They are designed to have a flat surface and plenty of room to bake one or more dozen cookies at one time.

Cooling Racks

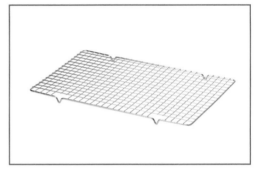

Once removed from the oven, baked goods need to cool. A cooling rack allows air to circulate around the food.

Round Cake Pans

Round cake pans often measure 8 or 9 inches in diameter and are usually used to make layer cakes. You need two round pans because cakes often consist of two layers, which should be baked at the same time.

Square Baking Pans

Square or rectangular baking pans are ideal for desserts such as cobblers. They can also be used for baked dishes such as eggplant parmesan.

Muffin Pans

A muffin pan has individual cups for baking muffins or cupcakes. A standard pan makes 12 muffins.

Pie Plates

Pie plates, also called pie pans, are for making all types of pies. Tempered glass pie plates distribute heat evenly for a nicely browned bottom crust.

Specialty Pans

A springform pan is round, with removable sides that make it easier to turn out delicate cakes without tearing them.

A tube pan, also known as an angel food or sponge cake pan, is a deep, round pan with a hollow tube in the center.

Loaf Pans

Loaf pans can be used to bake bread, pound cakes, and meatloaf. They may be made of metal or heat-proof glass.

Kitchen Helpers

- Parchment paper is a grease-resistant paper that comes in easy-to-use rolls. Use it to line baking sheets to prevent cookies from sticking.

- Oven mitts are often made of padded cloth, but silicone oven mitts protect hands at temperatures of 400 degrees or more. When choosing a mitt, be sure it fits properly so that you can get a good grip on pans and they do not slip.

Small Appliances

Every kitchen has large appliances such a refrigerator and an oven. A well-equipped kitchen will also have small appliances to help you chop, blend, and mix your ingredients.

Food Processors

A food processor makes quick work of many tasks, including making pie dough, chopping nuts, slicing vegetables, and grating cheese or carrots. Food processors can also blend and pureé ingredients.

Blenders

An immersion blender is a small hand-held blender. It is handy for small jobs because you can place it directly into a bowl or saucepan to pureé ingredients.

A countertop blender can perform heavy-duty tasks such as chopping ice, grinding fruit, and blending smoothies.

Mixers

A hand mixer, or beater, is useful for light tasks such as beating egg whites, whipping cream, and mixing cake batter.

A stand mixer doesn't have to be held. It is perfect for jobs that can take a long time, such as mixing bread dough or beating egg whites until they are stiff.

Measuring Ingredients

You may have heard someone say that a recipe takes a "pinch" of this or a "dash" of that. To prepare food properly with the best results every time, it is better to measure your ingredients carefully.

Dry and Semi-Solid Ingredients

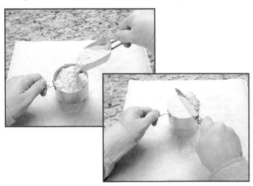

For dry ingredients such as flour or sugar, use a scoop to fill the correct cup. Move the straight edge of a table knife across the rim of the cup to level the ingredients.

To measure semi-solid ingredients such as peanut butter, use a spatula to fill the correct cup, pressing the ingredient down to remove any air pockets. Move the straight edge of a table knife across the rim of the cup to level the ingredients.

Liquid Ingredients

Place the cup on a level surface and pour the liquid in until it reaches the measurement you want.

Measuring Spoons

Measuring spoons may be used for dry and semi-solid ingredients as well as liquid ingredients. After you fill the spoon, use the straight edge of a table knife to level dry or semi-solid ingredients.

Reading a Recipe

A recipe is a set of instructions for preparing food. Once you know how to read a recipe, you can cook just about anything! Before you begin to cook, read the recipe from beginning to end. Be sure you have enough time to finish the job and that you have all of the tools and ingredients you will need on hand.

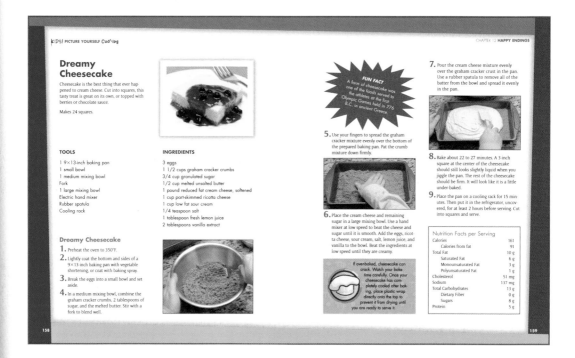

Ingredient List

The ingredient list tells you what ingredients are included in the recipe and how much of each you will need. Some may be listed as "optional." That means you don't have to use them, but you can if you like.

The way that the ingredient is listed can give important information about preparation. For example, "1 cup of chopped walnuts" is a cup of walnuts that have been chopped before measuring. If it is listed as "1 cup of walnuts, chopped" it means that the walnuts should be measured whole and then chopped.

Getting Started

Before you begin to cook, collect all of the ingredients, tools, appliances, and cookware you will need. Measure the ingredients and prepare them as listed in the recipe. Most recipes list things in the order they will be used, so it saves time to set them up on the kitchen counter in that order. If you need to preheat the oven, do so before you begin to mix and measure.

Servings

Most recipes list the number of servings that the recipe will make. If you need half the number of servings the recipe will make, you can divide the amounts of ingredients in half. If you need more, you can double or even triple the amounts of the ingredients. Remember that making extra may also require adjusting the cooking time.

Serving Suggestions and Recipe Variations

Some recipes include suggestions for how to serve the dish you are making or what to serve with it. Sometimes the recipe includes ideas for different ingredients or alternate ways of preparing the dish. It can be fun to try variations on a recipe. You might like the new way even better.

Standard Ingredients (In This Book)

Some ingredients come in different forms, which can make a difference in how the dish turns out. Unless the recipe says otherwise, here is a list of what the recipes in this book call for:

- Milk: use 1%

- Pepper: use freshly ground black pepper

- Eggs: use large eggs

- Butter: use unsalted butter

- Salt: use table salt

- Broth: use low sodium canned broth

- Lemon or lime juice: use freshly squeezed juice

Directions

It is important to read the directions for a recipe carefully and follow them in the correct order. If you're using a pot or pan, don't cover it unless the directions say to do that. When you are cooking on the stove, follow the suggestions for setting the burner temperature.

If you are using the oven, make sure it has reached the correct temperature before you put the food in. Always use the center rack unless the recipe says otherwise.

Oven temperature gauges are not always consistent. You might want to purchase an inexpensive oven thermometer. Remember that cooking times may be a little different for different ovens. Many recipes give a range of cooking times, and it is up to the cook to decide when the food is ready. The recipe may give hints to help you, such as, "bake until lightly browned," or "bake until a toothpick comes out clean." Start checking the food for doneness at the earliest time given in the recipe.

Nutritional Information

Some recipes give nutritional information for each dish. It may include the amount of calories, fat, carbohydrates, dietary fiber, and protein in each serving. This information is important for people who are on special diets.

CHAPTER 2

Fresh, tasty, simple foods are combined and flavored with spices and herbs to make the great-tasting recipes you'll find later in this book. Vegetables, fruit, grains, meats, fish, and chicken are cooked or combined to create dishes that will make you the hero of the dinner table. Milk, eggs, and cheese go into sauces. Here are some facts about the various ingredients you'll use as you begin cooking.

Herbs and Spices

Much of the flavor in a recipe comes from the herbs and spices that you include. Herbs are plants with fragrant leaves or stems that are used to flavor food. Herbs may be dried or fresh. Spices usually come from plants and may be made from bark, roots, fruit, flowers, seeds, berries, or pods. They may be sold whole or ground as a powder. They are almost always used dried.

Tip

Some herbs taste best when they are used fresh rather than dried. When using fresh herbs, wash and dry them carefully before you add them to food. Dried herbs and spices can lose flavor over time. To preserve them for as long as possible, store them in an air-tight container and away from direct sunlight and heat. Mark the container with the date that it is first opened. Most dried herbs and spices last no longer than one year after opening.

Spices

Spice	Form and Descriprion

Allspice

 The ground powder tastes like a blend of cinnamon, nutmeg, and cloves. It is used in baked goods.

Ancho Chili Powder

 Mildly hot and sweet flavor. Used in chili, marinades, soups, and stews.

Cayenne Pepper

 Made from spicy chili peppers. Used in salsas and marinades. Cayenne pepper is very hot and must be used carefully.

Cinnamon

 Sweet, woodsy flavor. Usually used in baked goods. Cinnamon sticks may be served in holiday drinks such as hot apple cider.

Cloves

 Dried, unopened flower buds from a tree, cloves have a strong, sweet flavor. They are used to flavor meats, such as ham, and for pickling vegetables.

Coriander Seed

 Warm, earthy flavor. Coriander is used in curries and in many Mexican foods.

Cumin

 Warm, nutty flavor. Used in fish, poultry, and beef dishes. Cumin is an ingredient in curry powder.

Curry Powder

 A mixture of spices such as turmeric and cumin. It ranges from mild to spicy and is used in curry, chicken, and rice dishes.

Spice	Form and Descriprion	Spice	Form and Descriprion
Dry Mustard 	Spicy, sharp flavor. Used in meat and vegetable dishes as well as marinades.	Pepper 	Peppercorns may be green, white, or black. Black is most common. Pepper is used in many dishes and is best when freshly ground.
Garlic Powder 	Dried, powdered garlic. Used in many types of dishes.	Red Pepper 	Hot, spicy flakes. Used in salsa, chili, and meat dishes.
Ginger 	Warm, tangy flavor. Used in sweet and savory dishes from desserts to meats and vegetables.	Turmeric 	Fragrant, earthy flavor. Used in curry, rice, and poultry dishes.
Nutmeg 	Sweet, spicy flavor. Used in baked goods, sauces, and soups. Best when freshly grated.	Vanilla 	Fragrant, sweet flavor. Commonly used as an extract to flavor desserts and baked goods.
Paprika 	Ranges from sweet to hot. Used in goulash, stews, rice dishes, and dips.		

Herbs

Herb	Form	Description
Basil	Fresh leaves	Grows in many varieties, such as lemon, herb, cinnamon, and spicy globe. Used in tomato sauce, pesto, and many Italian dishes.
Bay	Whole fresh Leaves	Used to flavor soups and stews. Bay leaves are removed from food before serving.
Chives	Leaves and flowers	Mild, onion-like flavor. Used in salads or as a garnish.
Cilantro	Fresh leaves and stems	Bright, citrus flavor. Used in salads and salsas. The seeds of cilantro are used as a spice called coriander.
Dill	Fresh leaves and stems	The feathery leaves are sometimes called dill weed. It is used in soups and fish dishes. The dill seeds are used as a pickling spice.
Marjoram	Fresh leaves	Sweet, woodsy flavor. Used in fish dishes, tomato sauces, and stews.
Oregano	Fresh leaves and flowers	Earthy flavor. Used in tomato sauce and meat dishes.
Rosemary	Fresh leaves	Pine flavor. Used in vegetables and grilled meat dishes.
Sage	Fresh leaves	Fragrant, mint flavor. Used in stuffing, poultry, and fish dishes.
Tarragon	Fresh leaves	Warm, slight licorice flavor. Used in sauces and roasted meats. Also used to flavor vinegars and mustards.
Thyme	Fresh leaves	Warm, citrus and mint flavor. Used with stews, fish, meat, and poultry dishes.

Ready for Rice

For nearly half of the world's population, rice is a part of daily life. In fact, thousands of varieties of rice are grown around the world.

FUN FACT

Rice is grown on every continent except Antarctica. It has been grown for food for as long as 7,000 years! In India, it is the first food that a new bride offers her husband and the first food that parents offer a newborn baby.

Types of Rice

Rice Type	Descriprion	Taste	Cooked Texture
White rice	White rice is what is left after the outer husk, bran, and germ are removed. A lot of the nutrients are removed at the same time, so white rice is usually enriched with nutrients.	Ranges from fragrant to bland	Soft but not mushy
Brown rice	Brown rice has only the outer husk removed. Because it still has the bran and the germ, brown rice has more fiber and certain nutrients than white rice.	Slightly nutty	Chewy, not completely soft
Basmati rice	A long-grained rice available in white and brown forms. Often used in Indian cooking.	Flavorful, slightly nutty	Light and grains are easily separated
Arborio rice	A short-grained rice available in white and brown forms. It has a high starch content and is usually used in sushi, risotto, and even some desserts.	May be slightly sweet	Moist and grains tend to stick together
Wild rice	Not a true rice, wild rice is a grain that comes from North American marsh grass. It is dark brown or black in color. It must be rinsed before cooking and is often packed as a mix with other varieties of rice.	Strong, nutty flavor	Very chewy

Perfect Pasta

Pasta is the Italian word for paste. It is also the name of one of the most popular food choices in the United States. Dried or fresh, pasta is a form of macaroni, spaghetti, or egg noodle, and it comes in more than 600 shapes. Pasta that needs to be twirled when eaten, like fettuccine, is often served with a thick sauce that sticks to the pasta. Thinner sauces are usually paired with tubular-shaped pasta, like penne, so the sauce can seep into the holes.

FUN FACT

Kids eat more pasta than any other age group. Their favorites are macaroni & cheese and spaghetti.

Pre-Stuffed Pasta

* Pre-stuffed pasta can be made fresh or purchased fresh or frozen. It can be filled with meat, cheese, shellfish, vegetables, and other stuffings.

* Shapes include ravioli (square or round), agnolotti (half-moons) and tortollini (ring-shaped twists).

Grain-Like Pasta

* Orzo is a grain-like pasta which looks much like rice. Orzo is great in soups or served as a side dish.

* Couscous is shaped like round barley. It is often used in North African and Middle Eastern stewed dishes, or as a base for salads.

Long Pasta

✳ Long pasta rounds, such as spaghetti, are usually served with sauces that stick to the strands, such as carbonara.

✳ Long, hollow tubes, such as bucatini, are often served with tomato-based sauces.

✳ Long, flat noodles, such as fettuccine, are excellent with creamy sauces, such as Alfredo.

✳ Pasta made with eggs, such as tagliatelle, are usually flat. Egg noodles often come in nests that are made by twisting the pasta into a coiled shape before it dries.

Tubular and Shaped Pasta

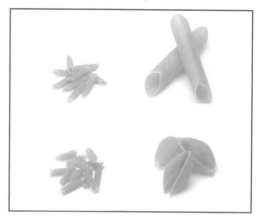

✳ Short pasta tubes, such as penne and macaroni, are often served with thick sauces or used in pasta casseroles.

✳ Larger tubes, such as cannelloni and manicotti, are often stuffed with meat or cheese mixtures and baked.

✳ Pastas are often named according to their shape. Some shaped pastas include fusilli (corkscrews) and orecchiette (little ears).

✳ Larger shaped pastas, such as jumbo shells (conchiglione), are often stuffed with meat or cheese mixtures and baked.

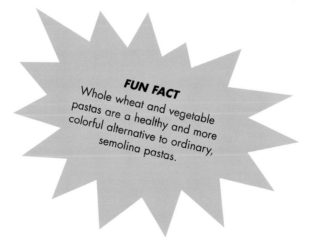

FUN FACT
Whole wheat and vegetable pastas are a healthy and more colorful alternative to ordinary, semolina pastas.

The Incredible Potato

Few foods are prepared in as many ways as the potato. The incredible potato may be mashed, baked, roasted, and fried. It shows up in side dishes, casseroles, stews, salads, French fries, pancakes, and chips. In fact, you could serve a different potato dish at breakfast, lunch, dinner, and snack time!

FUN FACT

The first time French fries were served in America was at a White House dinner given in 1802 by President Thomas Jefferson. They were a big hit, and today Americans eat about two million tons of them a year.

Selecting Potatoes

When you are getting ready to cook a potato, pick it up and feel it. It should be firm with no soft spots. If you are making a recipe that calls for several potatoes, be sure those you choose are roughly the same size so that they will cook evenly, or cut them into chunks of approximately the same size.

FUN FACT

Russet potato
A russet potato is a large potato that is often baked in the skin. It may also be used for potato mashing, roasting, and frying.

White potato
A white potato has a thin skin. It is an all-purpose potato used for boiling, frying, and baking.

Red potato
Red potatoes are round and fairly smooth. They are best for steaming, roasting, boiling, and pan-frying.

Yellow potato
Yellow potatoes, such as the Yukon Gold variety, have a naturally sweet, buttery flavor. They are great for mashing and roasting.

Preparing Potatoes

Potato skin is nutrient-packed. Remember that potatoes are a root crop and the edible part grows underground. If you plan to cook them with the skin on, first scrub them under running water with a stiff kitchen brush.

If you choose to peel the potato, you can easily remove the skin with a vegetable peeler or a paring knife.

The bud or sprout of a potato is called an eye. When you peel a potato, remove each eye with the tip of a vegetable peeler or with a paring knife.

Exceptional Eggs

If you want to bake a cake, some cookies, or a yummy omelet, you have to break some eggs. So give your eggs a break today! You can test a raw egg for freshness by placing it in a glass of water. A fresh egg will sink to the bottom. An older egg will float. That is because as it ages, some of the egg's moisture is replaced by air.

FUN FACT

Eggs come conveniently packaged in a leak-proof shell that is usually white or brown. The breed of the hen that laid the egg determines the shell color. For example, hens with white feathers and ear lobes lay white eggs. Hens with red feathers and ear lobes lay brown eggs. The color of the yolk inside the egg is determined by the hen's diet. Hens that eat grass, alfalfa, and yellow corn lay eggs with darker yolks than wheat-fed hens.

Easy-to-pour liquid eggs are a substitute for fresh eggs. You can find liquid whole eggs, egg whites, and egg yolks in the refrigerated section of your grocery store.

About Eggs

✳ Eggs contain plenty of vitamin A and D and other nutrients such as iron and calcium. They also contain all nine amino acids, which makes eggs a complete protein.

✳ The average egg contains about 70 calories.

Storing Eggs

✳ Always refrigerate your eggs until you are ready to use them. They spoil quickly if left at room temperature for more than an hour or two.

Grade and Size

✳ Eggs are usually packaged by the dozen according to size. They may be extra large to small. The size is determined by how much the average dozen weighs.

✳ Unless the recipe calls for a different size, use large eggs for cooking and baking.

✳ The eggs you find at the grocery store are usually graded AA (the highest quality) and A (good quality). The biggest difference between the two is price.

Fruits and Vegetables

Packed with vitamins and minerals, fruits and vegetables are an important part of any meal. Sometimes they play a supporting role as a flavoring or side dish. Sometimes they are the star!

FUN FACT
Bananas are the most popular fruit in the United States. They are actually the world's largest herb, and belong to the same family as lilies, orchids, and palms.

Selecting Fruit

Choose fruit that feels heavy for its size and does not have any cuts, bruises, or signs of mold. Fruit that is in season or fruit from a local farmer's market is likely to be fresh and tasty.

Ripening Fruit

If you find that the fruit you want to use is not quite ripe, you can sometimes speed up the process with a brown paper bag. Place the fruit in a paper bag with several pencil-sized holes in it. Loosely close the top of the bag. Place the bag on a counter at room temperature. Check each day until the fruit is ripe enough to use.

Cleaning Fruit

Always wash fruit before you eat it. Even if you plan to peel or cut the fruit, you should wash it first because bacteria on the outside can be transferred to the inside by a peeler or knife.

Selecting Vegetables

When you are choosing vegetables, freshness is the key. For vegetables such as broccoli, peppers, and asparagus, look for bright colors. For vegetables such as celery, carrots, and peas, you want them to be crisp. Those such as zucchini and cucumber should be firm with no soft spots. Choosing vegetables that are in season or locally grown is another way to ensure that you have the freshest ingredients.

Storing Vegetables

Your vegetables will stay fresh longer if you store them dry without washing them first. They will keep well in the crisper drawer of the refrigerator. Some root vegetables, such as potatoes and rutabagas, should be stored in a cool, dark place.

Cleaning Vegetables

When you are ready to prepare vegetables to eat, the first thing you have to do is wash them well. To clean most vegetables, rinse them under cold running water or in a bowl of fresh water. Use a vegetable brush to scrub firm-skinned vegetables such as potatoes. On a clean cutting board, use a paring knife to trim away any areas that are cracked, bruised, or spoiled.

FUN FACT
When you think of Halloween and Jack-o-Lanterns, do pumpkins come to mind? Actually, the first Jack-o-Lanterns were carved in Ireland and Scotland, and they were usually made from the rutabaga, a large cousin of the turnip.

FUN FACT

Lettuce is a member of the sunflower family.

Selecting Salad Greens

Salad greens are available in several forms. You can choose heads of lettuce, bunches of greens, or even pre-washed and pre-mixed bags of salad greens. When you are preparing your salad, look closely at the greens to be sure they are crisp and fresh. Remove any leaves that are wilted, limp, browned, or mushy. Darker green vegetables, such as kale or spinach, contain more nutrients than lighter-colored varieties like iceberg lettuce.

Cleaning Salad Greens

It is important to clean salad greens very well. Nothing will ruin a salad more than a gritty texture. To clean greens, fill a large bowl with cool fresh water. Place the greens in the water and swirl them around, allowing any dirt to settle to the bottom of the bowl. Remove the greens, rinse them under running water, and then dry them in a salad spinner. For greens that can be sandy, such as spinach, change the water in the bowl once or twice until no grit sinks to the bottom of the bowl.

Storing Salad Greens

Salad greens need air and moisture, but don't wash greens before storing them. Wrap bunches of greens such as watercress or arugula in damp paper towels and place them in unsealed plastic bags in the refrigerator. The bags help to keep the greens from drying out and wilting. Store herbs in the refrigerator. First cut off a little of the stem and put the cut ends in a glass of water with a plastic bag over the green leafy part.

Types of Lettuce

Boston and Bibb Lettuce
Both Boston and Bibb lettuces have floppy, light green leaves, loosely attached to the head. The leaves are tender with a mild, slightly sweet flavor.

Leaf Lettuce
Leaf lettuce refers to several types that grow loosely on stems rather than in heads. The colors of leaf lettuce range from bright green to deep red. The texture of the leaves may be smooth or ruffled. The flavor is often delicate and mild.

Iceberg Lettuce
This well-known lettuce is used for salads and sandwiches. It has crisp, pale-green leaves that wrap tightly around the head. The flavor of the leaves is very mild.

Romaine Lettuce
This familiar lettuce is known for its long leaves, which are tightly packed and joined on a stem. The leaves vary from deep green on the outside to yellow green at the center, or heart. Romaine is the lettuce used in Caesar salads.

Other Greens

Arugula
Arugula is slightly bitter and peppery. It works well with a mild-flavored lettuce.

Belgian Endive
Belgian endive comes in a tightly packed, pale yellow and white head that is longer than it is wide.

Frisee
This slightly bitter salad green has frilly leaves that add an interesting look and flavor to a mixed salad.

Radicchio
Radicchio has deep magenta leaves that come in a tightly formed head. It adds tangy flavor and bright color to salads.

Spinach
The dark green leaves of spinach may be oval and smooth or large and bumpy. It is very flavorful and packed with calcium, iron, and vitamins.

Watercress
Watercress has a peppery flavor and leaves that are shaped like clover. It makes a nice addition to mild salads.

CHAPTER 3

Learning the right way to do everyday tasks in the kitchen will make you a better cook. A good cook masters the basic techniques of food preparation. One of the most basic skills is slicing food into flat pieces of the same size and thickness. In addition to slicing, dicing, and chopping, you will learn in the following pages how to master breading, marinating, and whipping too! Mastering these basic techniques will help you to be a skilled cook.

Getting Ready

Slicing

SLICING TECHNIQUES

1. First cut a flat surface to make the food you are cutting easier and more stable to work with. Cut a lengthwise slice close to the outer edge of what you are cutting (shown here is a sweet potato being sliced). Place the cut side flat on the cutting board.

2. Hold food with your fingertips curled under and away from the blade of the knife. Do not lift the blade of the knife higher than your first knuckle so that it is always under control.

3. You may slice lengthwise or widthwise, but be sure that the cuts are evenly spaced.

4. When you feel comfortable with your technique, you may want to try making diagonal slices. This method is good for slicing vegetables such as cucumbers.

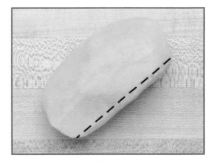

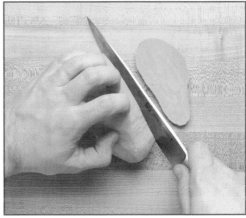

Tip

When slicing food, be sure that you are using the correct knife for the job and that the knife blade is sharp. A dull knife can lead to accidents.

Dicing

Recipes for salsas, soups, and stews sometimes ask for vegetables to be diced. That means that they are cut into small cubes that are the same size on all sides.

DICING TECHNIQUES

1. First cut a flat surface to make the food easier to work with by cutting a lengthwise slice close to the outside edge of the food. Place the item cut side down on the cutting board.

2. Make lengthwise cuts about 1/4 to 1/2 inch apart to create slices. Keep the food together in the order the slices were cut.

3. Stack and line up the edges of 3 or 4 slices. Holding the stack with one hand, make lengthwise cuts 1/4 to 1/2 inch apart to create sticks.

4. Repeat step 3 for the remaining slices.

5. Position the sticks in stacks of 3 or 4 and line up the edges. Holding the stacks with one hand, cut 1/4- to 1/2-inch slices across the width of the food. This is the last cut, and you will have evenly diced food.

6. Repeat step 5 with the rest of the sticks.

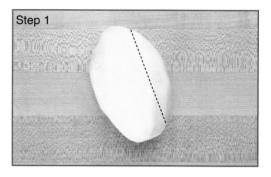

Step 1

Step 2

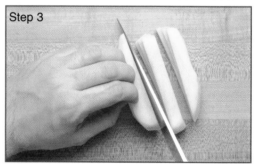

Step 3

Step 5

Chopping

One of the most familiar kitchen sounds is that of a knife chop, chop, chopping on a cutting block. Chopping is a skill that does not have to be too precise. From meats and herbs to vegetables and nuts, it is not hard to prepare a mound of food for a tasty dish.

FUN FACT

The ulu, a knife with a curved blade, is becoming a common tool in many modern kitchens. It is handy for chopping herbs. The original ulu was used by the Inuit women of the North American Arctic. They used it to cut food, give haircuts, and even trim blocks of snow to build igloos.

Fine Chopping

* Fine chopping is called mincing. Minced food is cut into tiny pieces of less than 1/4 inch.

* While any food can be finely chopped, it is usually used for herbs, nuts, and garlic.

* To mince an object, you cut it into thin pieces and then cut across the pieces to make smaller pieces. Keep the tip of the knife on the cutting board to keep control as you cut.

* Gather the chopped food into a pile and continue to chop until it is the size you want.

Coarse Chopping

* Coarse chopping, or rough chopping, is the process of cutting food into bite-sized pieces, usually about 3/4 inch or more.

* Carrots, celery, and potatoes are often coarsely chopped.

* It is not important that the pieces be exactly the same size or shape, but do try to keep the pieces as equal as possible.

Julienne Cuts

If you like shoestring potatoes or carrot salad, this is the cut for you. You will need a steady hand, but with practice you will be able to cut thin strips the size of matchsticks.

Creating Julienne Cuts

If the vegetable you want to cut needs to be peeled, trim and peel it before you slice.

When preparing long, slender vegetables, such as carrots or zucchini, cut them in half length-wise first so that you can place the flat side down on the cutting board. The vegetable will be more stable.

1. Make lengthwise cuts about 1/8 inch apart to create slices. Keep the slices together in the order they were cut.

2. Stack and line up the edges of 3 or 4 slices. Holding the stack with one hand, make lengthwise slices about 1/8 inch apart to create the thin julienne cuts.

3. Repeat step 2 for the remaining slices.

4. Gather the julienne sticks, line up the edges, and cut them to the length you want. Many recipes suggest that julienne cut vegetables should be about 2 inches long.

> Before cutting any vegetable, be sure that your knife and cutting board are clean and dry. Do not cut vegetables on a cutting board that is used for cutting meat.

Step 1

Step 2

Step 4

Pounding Meat

Pounding is often used to flatten boneless chicken breasts and thick slices of beef or pork. Pounding makes the meat more tender and allows it to cook quickly and evenly.

How to Pound Meat

1. Carefully wash the meat mallet and cutting board before you begin.

2. Place a piece of meat, such as a boneless chicken breast, between two sheets of plastic wrap or parchment paper on the cutting board.

3. Firmly hammer the center of the meat with the flat side of the meat mallet to flatten it. Continue hammering outward from the middle until the entire piece is the same thickness.

4. Stop every so often to check the thickness. Be careful not to pound the meat too thin or it might tear.

5. Pounding breaks down the connective tissue in the meat, making it more tender. Chicken is likely to need less pounding than beef or pork. For the toughest cuts of meat, use the rough side of the meat mallet.

Step 2

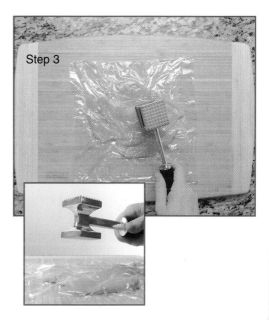

Step 3

If you do not have a meat mallet, or meat tenderizer, you can pound meat with a rolling pin or even the bottom of a heavy saucepan.

Breading

Breading is a simple technique in which you coat meat and vegetables that are juicy on the inside with crispy crunchy crusts. You can use seasoned bread crumbs, cornmeal, cracker crumbs, or even chopped nuts in the breading mixture.

How to Bread Meat

1. To prepare to bread meats or vegetables, set up three low containers in a row. (Square baking pans work well.) The first container is for a seasoned flour mixture, such as 1/2 cup whole wheat flour, 1 teaspoon salt, and 1/2 teaspoon pepper. The second container is for an egg wash made up of 1 egg beaten with 2 teaspoons of water. The third container is for a breading mixture of your choice.

2. Place the food to be breaded, such as a boneless chicken breast, in the seasoned flour, and coat it well on all sides. Lift the breast out and shake off any excess flour.

3. Dip the chicken in the egg wash. Be sure it is completely coated. Lift it out and let any excess egg drip off.

4. Place the chicken in the breading mixture. Heap the mixture on top so that the chicken is covered. Press down to make sure the mixture sticks to the chicken.

5. Place the breaded chicken breast on a plate covered in waxed paper. Repeat steps 2 to 4 for each chicken breast. When you have finished breading, place the chicken in the refrigerator for 20 minutes before cooking. This will help the breading to stay in place.

Step 1.

Step 3.

Step 2.

Step 4.

Use one hand for dipping food in dry ingredients and the opposite hand for wet ingredients. For example, use your right hand to place the food in the flour and the bread crumbs. Use you left hand for dipping the food in the egg mixture. This will help keep your fingers from getting gooey.

Marinating

If you would like to add extra flavor or a little zing to a meat or seafood dish, marinating the meat may do the trick. Marinating is the process of soaking the food in a liquid before cooking. Resealable plastic bags are ideal for holding marinating foods, but you can use a glass or ceramic bowl if you like.

About Marinades

❄ There are many types of marinades. Most contain an acid ingredient such as vinegar, citrus juice, yogurt, buttermilk, or wine.

❄ Salt, herbs, spices, oil, or sugar are often added to marinades to give food more flavor.

How to Marinate

1. Place the food you want to marinate in a plastic bag with the marinade. Squeeze the air out of the bag and seal the top. Squish the marinade around so that it coats the food evenly.

2. Place the bag in a pan in the refrigerator. Turn the bag every 30 minutes or so. You can marinate foods for a couple of hours before cooking or overnight. Follow the directions in each recipe for best results.

3. When you are ready to prepare your meal, remove the food from the bag and dispose of the marinade.

Acidic Ingredients

Flavoring Ingredients

MILK

YOGURT

salt

When you are marinating food, be sure to keep it in the refrigerator so that bacteria will not be able to grow. Marinating tougher cuts of beef overnight can help to make the meat more tender.

Whipping

Do you like a dollop of whipped cream to top off dessert? How about a yummy layer of meringue on a slice of pie? Whipping adds air to foods, such as cream or egg whites, and makes them light and fluffy.

Whipping by Hand

✳ To whip by hand, the best tool to use is a large balloon whisk.

✳ When whipping ingredients, tilt the bowl toward you slightly. Stir the mixture very quickly so that the whisk breaks the surface and adds air to the mixture.

✳ Whipping by hand takes a lot of effort. It takes about 100 stirs by hand to equal 1 minute of whipping with an electric mixer.

In some cultures, it is traditional to mix whipped cream in coffee and other drinks. Just say mit schlag!

©istockphoto.com/Christine Balderas

©istockphoto.com/Robert Linton

Whipping with an Electric Mixer

- Using an electric mixer is easier than whipping ingredients by hand, but you must be careful not to over-whip. If you whip the cream too much, you'll make butter!
- For the best results, set the mixer to the highest setting.
- When whipping egg whites, be sure that the bowl and beaters are very clean and dry. The egg whites should be at room temperature. The best bowl to use is an unlined copper bowl.
- When whipping cream, be sure that the cream, bowl, and beaters are all chilled.

Tip

Recipes may call for cream or egg whites that have been whipped to the "soft peak" or "stiff peak" stage. To check this, lift the whisk or beaters out of the mixture to form mounds. Smooth mounds with peaks that droop over are soft peaks. Firm mounds that end in a point that stays up are stiff peaks. It is better to under-whip slightly than to over-whip.

©istockphoto.com/Sandra O'Claire

Whipped cream is good atop hot drinks, and it's the finishing touch on all sundaes.

©istockphoto.com/Sandra O'Claire

CHAPTER 4

Food comes to us from trees, the garden, from animals and forests, and before we begin to cook, a food item often requires some preparation. It has to be cleaned, peeled, or cut up in a certain way. Seeds must be removed from some vegetables and eggs have to be taken out of their shells. This chapter is all about the prep work that must be done before you turn on the stove or mixer or begin stirring a pot of soup.

Peel and Prep

Peel and Seed Tomatoes

If you want to add tomatoes to a salad, all you have to do is slice, dice, or chop them. When making a sauce, puree, or soup, it is likely that you will have to peel and seed the tomatoes.

Before placing a tomato in boiling water to peel it, cut a shallow X at the bottom of the tomato. The skin will separate at the X and you will have a place to start to peel.

Peel a Tomato

Tools: vegetable peeler or paring knife

1. The best way to peel a tomato is to dip it in boiling water to loosen the skin. Bring a medium saucepan half-filled with water to a rapid boil with the lid on. Fill a large bowl halfway with cold water and several ice cubes.

2. Holding the tomato in one hand, remove the core and stem using a paring knife.

3. Remove the lid from the pot of boiling water. Using a slotted spoon or tongs, carefully lower the tomato into the boiling water.

4. Leave the tomato in the boiling water for 20 or 30 seconds, depending on its size.

5. Using the slotted spoon or tongs, remove the tomato and place it in the bowl of ice water for 1 minute.

6. Once the tomato has cooled, take it out of the water and dry it with a paper towel. Beginning at the bottom, peel the tomato.

7. If the skin is still difficult to peel, repeat steps 3 through 6.

Seed a Tomato

You can seed a tomato with or without the skin on.

Tools: chef's knife, small spoon

1. Using a sharp knife, cut the tomato in half widthwise.

2. Gently squeeze each half over a bowl to remove the seeds. Scoop out any leftover seeds with a small spoon.

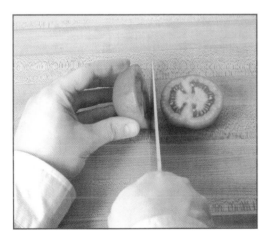

Chop Onions

The most difficult part of chopping an onion is the way it makes your eyes water. To avoid teary eyes, chill onions for about 1 hour in the refrigerator or 10 minutes in the freezer before chopping.

Dice an Onion

Tools: chef's knife

Store the trimming and papery skin of an onion in a plastic freezer bag in your freezer. Add them to the pot when you are preparing vegetable stock. They will add plenty of flavor and yellow onions will give a nice, golden color to the stock.

1. Lay the onion on its side and slice off the top. Do not slice off the root end. Cut the onion in half lengthwise.

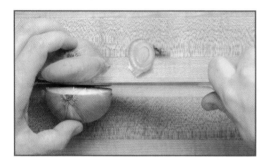

5. Repeat steps 3 and 4 with the other half of the onion.

6. To make larger pieces of onion, make the cuts in steps 3 and 4 farther apart. To mince the onion, make cuts in steps 3 and 4 closer together.

2. Take off the papery skin and any brown or spotted layers. Lay each onion half on a cutting board, cut side down.

3. Make 2 horizontal cuts within 1/2 inch of the root end. Make several lengthwise cuts through the onion about 1/4 inch apart. Do not cut through the root end.

4. Make several widthwise cuts through the onion, about 1/4 inch apart, until you reach the root end. Discard the root end.

Diced

Minced

Peel and Mince Garlic

If you want to bring out the flavor and nutrients in a clove of garlic, you need to mince it. The more you cut garlic, the more oil, and flavor, is released.

Peel a Garlic Clove

Tools: chef's knife

1. Separate a clove of garlic from the bulb. Remove any loose papery skin and place the garlic on a clean cutting board.

2. Place the flat side of a chef's knife on top of the garlic clove. Using the heel of your hand, firmly press down on the blade. Peel away the papery skin.

3. Trim off the root end and remove any brown spots from the clove.

Mince a Garlic Clove

Tools: chef's knife

1. Place a peeled clove on a cutting board. Using a chef's knife, make thin slices width-wise across the clove.

2. Holding the knife handle in one hand, spread the fingers of your other hand on top of the blunt back edge of the blade.

3. Moving the handle up and down, gently rock the sharp edge of the knife on the cutting board to finely chop the garlic into tiny pieces.

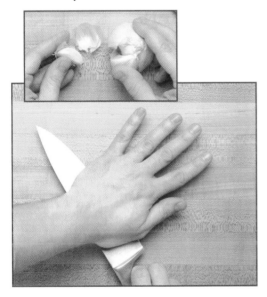

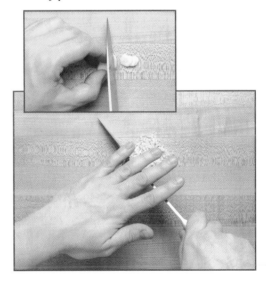

To separate garlic cloves quickly, place the whole garlic bulb, root side down, on a cutting board. Push down hard on the bulb with both hands until the cloves snap apart.

Prepare Mushrooms

Mushrooms are great in everything from omelets and soups to stir-fries and salads. They can be eaten raw or cooked. They can even be stuffed to make a tasty appetizer.

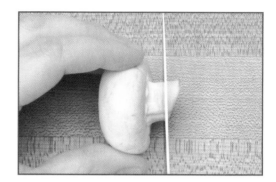

Some cooks like to use a soft brush to clean mushrooms. You can buy a special brush, but a soft, child-sized toothbrush works just as well.

Clean Mushrooms

Tools: soft brush, paper towels

Mushrooms are often flecked with dirt and should be cleaned carefully before using.

1. Lightly rinse each mushroom under cold running water. Use your fingers or a soft brush to gently loosen dirt.

2. Place the clean mushrooms on a paper towel on the counter. Gently blot them dry with another paper towel.

Slice Mushrooms

Tools: paring knife

1. Use a paring knife to cut off the bottom of the mushroom stem.

2. Place the mushroom on a clean cutting board, cap side down.

3. Slice the mushroom into pieces that are about 1/4 inch thick.

Seed and Peel Avocados

Avocados may be served raw, sliced in salads, or mashed in guacamole and salad dressings. Before you can use the soft, buttery flesh of the avocado, you have to remove the hard skin covering and large seed.

A cut avocado browns easily. To help prevent it from discoloring, brush avocado slices with fresh lemon juice.

Seed and Peel an Avocado

Tools: chef's knife, teaspoon

1. Using a chef's knife, slice completely around the avocado lengthwise. The large, hard seed in the center will keep the knife from slicing all the way through.

2. Hold both halves and gently twist them in opposite directions until they separate. One side will contain the seed. Set that side on the cutting board with the seed facing up.

3. Lightly strike the sharp edge of the knife into the seed. Gently turn the knife until the seed releases from the avocado. Use a dish towel to safely pull the seed away from the knife.

4. Gently slide a teaspoon between the flesh of the avocado and the skin all the way around. Lift the flesh out. Repeat this step with the other half of the avocado.

Peel and Core Apples

A crisp, juicy apple is a wonderful snack just the way it is. It is also a tasty treat in apple pie, apple cobbler, or a cool, crisp fruit salad. To prepare apples for many different dishes, you have to peel and core them. To core an apple means to remove the center and the seeds. The same technique you use for an apple works just as well for pears.

Peel Apples

Tools: vegetable peeler or paring knife

1. Wash the apple before you begin. Inspect the fruit to be sure that it has no soft or brown spots. Holding the apple in one hand, pull the blade of a vegetable peeler from the top of the fruit to the base.

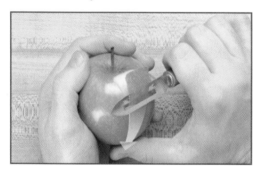

2. Rotate the fruit slightly and repeat step 1. Continue rotating and peeling until you have removed the skin of the entire apple.

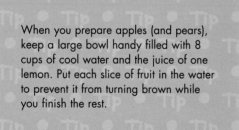

When you prepare apples (and pears), keep a large bowl handy filled with 8 cups of cool water and the juice of one lemon. Put each slice of fruit in the water to prevent it from turning brown while you finish the rest.

Core Apples

Tools: chef's knife

1. Place the peeled apple upright on a clean cutting board. Using a chef's knife, cut one side from the apple, slicing close to the core.

2. Rotate the apple 1/4 turn and repeat step 1. Continue to rotate and cut until you have 4 pieces of fresh apple with no seeds or core. Discard the core. Now you are ready to chop, slice, or dice the fruit.

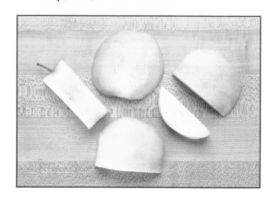

Zest and Grate Citrus

Did you know that you can eat the peel of a lemon? The tangy peel adds extra taste and vitamin C to your recipes. Thin strips of peel from citrus fruits, such as lemons, limes, and grapefruit, is called *zest*. Citrus zest makes an excellent garnish. Another way to add citrus flavor to your dishes is to grate the tangy peel.

Zesting Citrus Fruit

Tools: handheld zester

1. Carefully rinse and dry the fruit, such as a lemon, and hold it in one hand. With the other hand, press the edge of the citrus zester at the top of the fruit.

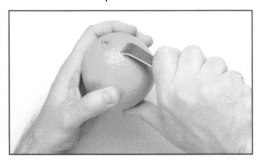

2. Using firm, even pressure, move the citrus zester downward to the bottom of the fruit.

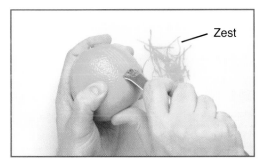

Zest

3. Rotate the fruit and repeat step 2 until you have enough zest.

Your recipe may call for citrus juice. There are many tools that are designed to juice citrus fruit. These include a hand-held tool called a *reamer*. You simply cut the fruit in half and hold one half over a bowl. Poke the pointed end of the reamer into the sliced side of the halved fruit and twist. Use a mesh strainer to catch any seeds.

Grating Citrus Peel

Tools: hand-held grater

1. Carefully rinse and dry the fruit, such as a lime. Hold a hand-held grater at an angle over a clean cutting board. Be sure the rough side of the grater is facing up and the top edge of the grater is resting on the board.

2. Rub the lime down against the rough side of the grater. Grate only the colorful part of the peel. The inner white layer, called the pith, is bitter.

3. Rotate the fruit and repeat step 2 until you have enough grated peel.

4. Store the fruit in the refrigerator to use for juice. Remember that it will dry out quickly without its peel. If you cannot use the juice within a day or 2, squeeze it into a plastic ice tray and freeze it.

Break and Separate Eggs

The incredible egg is a wonderful and versatile ingredient. Some recipes call for the whole egg. Others require just the white or just the yolk. Separating the egg yolk from the white is an important skill. Even a drop of egg yolk can prevent egg whites from whipping properly. A tiny piece of eggshell in an omelet can be very unpleasant. So it is time to get cracking and master the art of breaking and separating eggs.

Raw egg yolks covered in plastic wrap will last about 3 days in the refrigerator. Raw egg whites stored the same way will last for about 4 days.

Break an Egg

Tools: small bowl

1. Place a small, clean bowl on the counter. Pick up an egg in one hand.

2. Gently tap the middle of the egg against the counter to create a crack in the shell. Don't use too much force or you can shatter the shell. This creates tiny bits that can get into your food.

3. Holding the egg with both hands over the bowl, gently place your thumbs slightly inside the crack.

4. Slowly pull the two halves of the shell apart. Allow the egg to drop into the bowl.

5. Do not break an egg directly over a bowl holding other ingredients. Bits of eggshell are easier to see and remove if you break the egg into an empty bowl first.

6. To remove eggshell from the bowl, use a knife to push the shell to the upper edge where you can pick it up.

Separate an Egg

Tools: three small bowls, egg separator (optional)

1. Place three small, clean bowls on the counter. Gently tap an egg on the counter to create a crack in the shell.

2. Hold the egg upright over the middle bowl. Slowly pull off the top half of the eggshell. Be sure the yolk stays in the bottom half. Some of the whites will fall into the bowl.

3. Carefully pass the yolk from one shell to the other so that most of the egg white falls into the bowl.

4. Pour the egg yolk into the second bowl. If you accidentally break the yolk, put it into the second bowl as quickly as possible so that no yolk gets into the whites.

5. If the egg white is completely free of yolk, pour it into the third bowl and continue to separate eggs by following steps 1 through 4.

An egg separator is a handy tool that does a lot of the work for you. Place the separator over the first bowl and crack the egg directly into the center of the separator. The egg whites will slide through the openings and into the bowl. The yolk stays in the separator. Pour the yolk into a second bowl before you separate the next egg.

Beat and Fold in Egg Whites

There is a secret ingredient in egg whites that puts the *yum* in lemon meringue pie and the *wow* in angel food cake. The secret ingredient is air, which makes egg whites fluffy. To get air into the whites, beat them slowly at first; then beat them quickly until they stiffen into peaks. Use the technique of *folding* to add the whites to another mixture without letting the air out.

FUN FACT

Farm fresh eggs take longer to form peaks because they have thicker whites. It is harder to beat the air into thick whites.

Beat Egg Whites

Tools: clean bowl, hand mixer, or stand mixer

1. Be sure there is no yolk in your egg whites. Place the whites in a clean, dry bowl and set the mixer on a medium speed.

2. When the whites become foamy, start to beat them quickly.

When you beat egg whites, you will get the best results if you use a copper bowl. Stainless steel, ceramic, and glass bowls work well, too. Never use a plastic or an aluminum bowl. Plastic bowls can have a slight greasy film that will prevent your whites from forming peaks. Aluminum may react to any acid added to the whites, turning them gray.

3. When the whites become smooth and shiny, lift the beaters to check for peaks. If the peaks droop, they are soft. If the peaks stand up straight, they are stiff.

Soft peaks

Adding a white powder called *cream of tartar* will make your egg whites fluffier and more stable. When the whites become foamy, add 1/8 teaspoon of cream of tartar for each egg white. *Do not use cream of tartar if you are using a copper bowl.*

4. If the recipe calls for sugar, add it gradually at the soft peak stage.

✳ If you beat the whites too much, they will dry out. It is better to under-beat them than to over-beat them. Use the egg whites immediately because they start to lose air as soon as you stop mixing.

FUN FACT
Cream of tartar is a fruit acid. It is processed from deposits left behind on the insides of wine barrels.

Stiff peaks

Fold in Beaten Egg Whites

Tools: clean spoon, large clean rubber spatula

✳ Beaten egg whites are delicate. Be sure that your utensils are clean and dry and work gently but quickly.

1. When they are ready to use, scoop a large spoonful of the beaten whites into the batter with which they will be combined. Stir well for about 1 minute to lighten the mixture.

2. Scoop the remaining egg whites on top of the batter.

3. In a circular motion, stir along the inside of the bowl with a wide spatula, going down to the bottom of the bowl.

4. As you continue to circle with the spatula, gently scoop some of the batter from the bottom of the bowl to the surface, folding it over the egg whites.

5. Give the bowl a 1/4 turn and repeat steps 3 and 4. Continue to fold until only a few streaks of egg white are visible. Use the batter immediately.

Working with Fresh Herbs

Dried herbs from a jar are easy to use, but fresh herbs are a wake up call for your taste buds. Many types of fresh herbs can be found in the produce section of grocery stores. Some are even easy to grow in pots near a sunny kitchen window. Some of the most popular herbs include thyme, parsley, cilantro, oregano, rosemary, and basil.

FUN FACT
Parsley is often used as a garnish, but don't leave it on the plate. Chewing parsley after a meal will freshen your breath.

Herbs with Hard Stems

Tools: colander, salad spinner

1. To remove the leaves of herbs with hard stems, such as rosemary and thyme, start with a single stem.

2. Hold the top of the stem with one hand. Using your other hand, pinch the stem between your thumb and index finger. Start just below where you are holding the stem.

3. Slide your pinched thumb and finger down the length of the stem and the leaves should come off easily.

4. Place the leaves in a colander and wash them gently under running water. Dry them in a salad spinner.

Fresh herbs may be milder than dried herbs, so you may need to add a little more if you are using fresh.

Herbs with Soft Stems

Tools: chef's knife

1. Herbs with soft stems, such as dill and tarragon, can be chopped without separating the leaves from the stems. Clean and dry the herbs carefully and place the entire bunch on a clean cutting board.

2. Cut the amount you will need from the bunch. Gather that amount in a tight bundle, and make widthwise cuts across the herbs. Continue to chop until you have the size you need.

Shaving Herbs

Tools: chef's knife

The leaves of bushy herbs, such as parsley and cilantro, can be shaved off their stems with a chef's knife.

1. Hold the whole bunch by the stems over a paper towel. Slide a chef's knife along the stems toward the leaves. Shave the leaves off the bunch in a smooth downward motion.

2. Turn the bunch and repeat step 2 until you have shaved off the amount of leaves you need.

3. Place the leaves in a colander and wash them gently under running water. Dry them in a salad spinner.

Chiffonade Cuts

Tools: chef's knife, colander, salad spinner

The leaves of broad-leafed herbs, such as basil and sage, can be cut into strips using a technique called *chiffonade.*

1. Clean and dry 5 or 6 leaves of the same size. Trim away the stem and stack the leaves on a clean cutting board.

2. Roll the leaves lengthwise into a tight bundle.

3. Cut very thin strips across the width of the bundle.

FUN FACT
Chiffonade is from a French term meaning "made of rags."

You can easily grow your own herbs on your kitchen windowsill.

©istockphoto.com/Rainforest Australia

You've assembled all your ingredients and measured the required amounts for your recipe. You've cleaned vegetables, peeled fruit, and cut everything into the size needed. It's time to turn on the stove and begin cooking!

Time to Cook

Stove and Oven Basics

Many wonderful meals begin on the kitchen stove, or range. The stove is a large appliance, usually with four or more burners. The burners provide the heat for boiling, simmering, frying, and other cooking techniques. Your stove may be gas or electric. Cooking methods and times mentioned in recipes will be the same for both.

The oven is the appliance used for baking, roasting, and broiling. It, too, can be gas or electric. The kitchen oven may be part of the stove, directly underneath the burners, or it may be completely separate from it.

Gas and Electric Stoves

There are some differences between gas and electric stoves. One thing to keep in mind is that electric stovetops change temperature more slowly than gas stovetops do. To reduce the heat on a pot of water over a gas burner, just turn down the gas. To reduce the heat on an electric burner, turn it down and remove the pot from the burner for a minute or two.

Electric stove

Gas stove

Stovetop Safety Tips

✳ Never leave a pot or pan on the stovetop unattended while the burner is on.

✳ Use the burner size that best fits the pot or pan you are using.

✳ Use oven mitts or potholders to handle pots and pans when you move them.

✳ Steam from cooking food can cause a burn. When you lift the lid of a pot or pan, lift it so that it opens away from you and the steam can escape safely.

✳ Keep pot and pan handles pointed toward the center of the stovetop. This keeps the handles out of the way while you are working.

Using Ovens

Sometimes your recipe will ask you to preheat the oven. That means that you should set the proper temperature on the oven and wait until it is reached before you put the food inside. Before you turn on the oven, check to be certain that it is empty. Move the oven rack while it is cool so that the pan or tray you are using fits where you want it.

Tips About Terms

Bake: Cook in dry heat. Bread, cakes, potatoes, and casseroles are baked.

Roast: Cook by exposure to radiant heat all around. Meat such as chicken or beef may be roasted.

Broil: Cook by direct exposure from a heat source. In an oven, the heat source comes from above. Fish is often broiled.

Simmer

When you boil a liquid on the stovetop, you get big rolling bubbles that pop quickly. Simmering is the stage just before boiling. When you simmer, you want small slowly rising bubbles that break gently at the surface. Dishes that are usually simmered are soups, stews, and sauces. Sometimes a recipe says to bring food to a boil then reduce the heat and let the liquid simmer for a while.

Simmering

1. To simmer food, add a liquid, such as broth, to a pot on the stove.

2. Heat the liquid until it boils with large bubbles quickly breaking at the surface of the liquid.

3. Carefully add the food you want to simmer in the pot. You don't want it to splash or splatter. The liquid may stop boiling when you add the food.

When simmering food, check the recipe to see if you should cover the pot or pan.

4. Allow the liquid to return to a boil. Then reduce the heat to simmer.

5. Check the food now and then to be sure it is simmering properly.

Cooking Time: Vegetables

Vegetables come in every size, shape, and color. They may be tender or crisp, sweet or spicy. You can use your imagination when preparing vegetables. Mash or roast sweet potatoes. Steam some summer squash or serve it in crisp raw slices. Think of the produce department at your local grocery store as an adventure. Prepare a vegetable from the following list or try something new!

Cooking Methods

❊ Boil vegetables by immersing them in boiling water in an uncovered pot. Boiling is easy, but vegetables can lose nutrients in the water.

❊ Steam vegetables in a steamer basket over boiling water in a covered container. Vegetables cooked this way retain their color, texture, and nutrients.

❊ Roast vegetables by tossing them with olive oil and seasonings, then placing them in the oven on an uncovered baking sheet.

The Internet is a great place to find out about new or unusual foods. A little surfing can help you learn about and find recipes for interesting vegetables such as fennel, okra, celeriac, rhubarb, parsnips, rutabagas, and kohlrabi. Look some of these vegetables up online or, better yet, find them in the produce department at your grocery store or at a farmer's market.

Vegetable	Boil or Steam	Roast	Doneness
Asparagus	5 to 8 minutes	5 to 10 minutes	Soft but not limp
Green Beans	4 to 8 minutes	Not recommended	Barely tender
Broccoli	5 to 7 minutes	5 to 10 minutes	Stalks are tender
Brussels Sprouts	8 to 15 minutes	20 to 30 minutes	Tender not mushy

Vegetable		Boil or steam	Roast	Doneness
	Cabbage	7 to 20 minutes	Not recommended	Tender not mushy
	Carrots (1-inch slices)	6 to 8 minutes	35 to 45 minutes	Tender not soft
	Cauliflower	5 to 6 minutes	whole 30 to 40 minutes cut into florets 15 to 20 minutes	Stems tender but firm
	Leeks	10 to 20 minutes	10 to 20 minutes	Tender not chewy
	Snow Peas	2 to 4 minutes	Not recommended	Crisp-tender
	Green Peas	2 to 4 minutes	Not recommended	Crisp-tender
	Potato (cubed)	20 to 25 minutes	40 to 60 minutes	Tender to center
	Summer Squash (cubed)	2 to 5 minutes	Not recommended	Crisp-tender
	Sweet Potato (cubed)	20 to 40 minutes	30 to 50 minutes	Tender to center
	Winter Squash (cubed)	20 to 30 Minutes	30 to 60 Minutes	Tender to center

Cooking Pasta

1. Fill a stockpot two-thirds full with cold water and then place the lid on the stockpot. Place a large colander in the sink for draining the pasta later.

2. Bring the water to a rapid boil with plenty of rolling bubbles. Remove the lid and add a tablespoon of salt to the water. Do not add oil to the water; if you do, the sauce will not stick to the pasta properly.

3. Add the pasta to the water and stir to keep it from sticking. Continue to stir until the water returns to a boil. Stir occasionally.

FUN FACT
October is National Pasta Month.

4. No matter what type of pasta you are using, you will find recommended cooking times on the package. Cook the pasta to the shortest time, then start checking to see if it is done.

5. Remove a piece of pasta from the stockpot. Be very careful to protect your hands with a mitt. Allow the pasta to cool for a couple of minutes, then bite into it.

6. It should be cooked so that it is still a little firm, but not crunchy. It should be soft enough not to stick to your teeth. This is called al dente. Once it reaches this stage, it is time to drain it in the colander in the sink. Remember that the boiling water and steam are very hot, so use mitts and pour slowly and carefully without splashing.

7. To serve the pasta with sauce, immediately put it in a serving bowl or on plates, then top it with sauce.

Sauté and Stir-Fry

To whip up a quick, delicious meal, try the simple techniques of sauté and stir-fry. Depending on the recipe, you can put together a meal in a single pan in under 30 minutes. Sautéing and stir-frying use oil to quickly cook small pieces of food, such as meat, onions, or vegetables, at high temperatures in a skillet or sauté pan.

Sautéing and Stir-Frying

To sauté or stir-fry, you must work quickly. Be sure to clean, slice, and chop all of your ingredients and measure all of your herbs and spices before you begin to cook.

1. Place a large sauté pan or wok over medium heat. Add 2 tablespoons of olive, safflower, or canola oil to the pan and allow it to become very hot.

2. Hot oil can splatter. Be very careful as you put the food you are cooking into the oil. Make sure the food has dried completely after you wash it. Water droplets can splatter and cause burns.

Pan frying is a cooking technique that is similar to sautéing, but the food is in larger pieces. For example, you would pan fry a whole, boneless chicken breast. You would sauté or stir-fry chopped pieces of chicken.

3. Allow the food to cook as you constantly toss it in the pan with a pair of flat-edged wooden spoons.

A traditional Asian pan called a *wok* is used for stir-frying. It is a deep pan with a curved surface that is wide at the top. It cooks chopped food very quickly in a small amount of hot oil.

4. Never leave a sauté pan unattended because the food cooks quickly and can burn easily. When the food is ready, remove it from the pan to a plate or bowl. Set the pan on a cool burner to allow it to cool before you wash it.

Stew

On a cold winter night, nothing tastes better than a warm, delicious serving of stew. The melt-in-your-mouth goodness is the result of using moist heat to slow cook ingredients such as vegetables, meat, poultry, or fish in a broth or other liquid.

When you are making a meat stew, you might decide to start by searing the meat. Simply add a little oil to a skillet over medium-high heat. Place the meat in the pan and cook it quickly until it has a slight crust on all sides. Searing seals in the meat's natural juices.

Stewing

1. To prepare a stew, place the sliced or chopped food in a Dutch oven or stew pot. Add any seasoning.

2. Add liquid such as water, juice, or broth. The liquid should just cover the food.

3. Place the pot on a burner at medium-high heat and bring the liquid to a boil.

4. If you are using a Dutch oven, place it in a preheated oven as directed in the recipe. If you are using a stew pot, reduce the heat and allow the stew to simmer on the stove-top until done. Stir occasionally to be sure the food isn't sticking to the bottom of the stew pot.

FUN FACT
One of the world's most beloved dishes is Irish Stew. It started out as a one-dish peasant meal made from tough cuts of meat that needed to be simmered for a long time. The stew also includes potatoes, onions, and a little beer or Irish whiskey. The alcohol is cooked away leaving only the flavor behind.

Roast

Roasting concentrates flavors in food. It is a simple method that gives meat, poultry, and fish a delicious crusty outside and a tender, juicy inside. Root vegetables, such as onions, potatoes, and carrots, release their natural sugars and turn a golden brown when roasted. Roasted food is cooked uncovered in the oven with little or no liquid.

Roasting

1. Preheat the oven to the temperature recommended in the recipe. Place the food in a roasting pan and put the pan in the preheated oven.

2. If you are roasting whole poultry (chicken or turkey), place it breast side up in the pan.

Drizzling pan juices or other liquids over foods as they roast is called *basting*. Usually, only poultry, such as turkey or chicken, is basted. The process helps to brown the skin evenly and keep it moist. Basting makes skin tender and juicy. If you like crispy skin, don't baste very much.

After meat has been roasted, it needs to rest on a cutting board for about 15 minutes before you slice it. The resting time allows the juices to seep through the meat and prevents it from becoming dry.

3. During roasting, use a meat thermometer to check the temperature at the center of red meat or poultry. Check the temperature at the thickest part of the meat and be sure not to let the thermometer touch any bones.

4. Meats continue to cook inside after they leave the oven. To avoid overcooking, remove the food from the oven when it is about 5 degrees less than the desired temperature.

5. Use tongs to move the meat to a cutting board to let it rest for about 15 minutes. Don't use a meat fork because juices will drain from any holes poked in the roast.

Baking Tips

Baking means cooking food in an oven using dry heat. Baking is part art and part science. You have to combine the right ingredients and measure and mix carefully. To bake successfully, you must use the right bakeware for the job and be sure that the oven is at the correct temperature. Your friends and family will appreciate your attention to detail when you bake a perfect loaf of bread, a scrumptious cake, or a tray of chewy cookies.

Ingredients

Always read the recipe carefully before you start to bake. Gather your ingredients and be sure they are prepared properly. For example, if a recipe calls for softened butter, take the butter out of the refrigerator so that it can reach room temperature. For room temperature eggs, let the eggs sit on the counter for about 20 or 30 minutes before using them.

Baking Tools and Pans

Collect the baking tools you will need, such as pans, whisks, spatulas, pastry brushes, and bowls. Use the size and type of pan called for in the recipe and prepare it as instructed. For example, a recipe may ask you to line a pan with parchment paper. If you need to grease a pan, use a pastry brush to lightly brush on oil or butter. If the recipe asks you to flour the pan after greasing it, sprinkle flour over the surface. Turn the pan upside down over the sink to tap out any excess flour.

Measure Carefully

You've probably heard cooks say to use a *bit* of this or a *pinch* of that, but measuring ingredients accurately is very important when you are baking. Make sure you are using the right tools for the ingredients. Use liquid measuring cups for wet ingredients such as milk or water. Use dry measuring cups for dry or semi-solid ingredients such as flour, sugar, or peanut butter.

Mix Carefully

Follow the instructions in the recipe for mixing times. You may want to use a timer to be sure you don't under- or over-mix ingredients. Some ingredients, such as baking powder, activate as soon as they are mixed in. Beaten egg whites start to lose air once you combine them with other mixtures. Work as quickly as possible so that all of the ingredients are at their peak.

Oven Temperatures

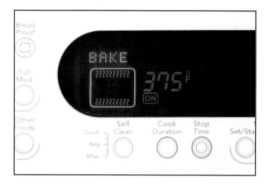

Allow the oven to preheat to the proper temperature for a few minutes before baking. Don't bake too many things at once. Too many pans will prevent the air from circulating around the oven as it should and the food won't bake evenly. Most ovens have a glass door and a light inside. Use these when you want to check on the food. Avoid opening the door during baking because this lets heat escape and the oven temperature to change. You should only open the oven door near the end of the baking time to check for doneness.

Cool Baked Goods

Always let your baked goods cool before you serve or taste them. Some goodies, such as brownies, may be served from the same pan in which they were baked. Simply set the pan on a cooling rack. Cakes and loaves should be removed from the pan. Set the pan on a cooling rack for about ten minutes then run a butter knife around the cake to release it from the sides of the pan. Place a plate on top and flip the pan over so that the cake is upside down on the plate. Flip the cake onto the cooling rack right side up and let it cool completely.

Recipes

And now—the recipes! These are tried and true, simple recipes that taste good, are easy to make, and will help you practice all the cooking skills we've been talking about so far. Your family will be impressed when you serve up any of these dishes. Turn the pages and learn how to make some totally tasty tidbits for everyone to enjoy!

CHAPTER 6

Appetizers, snacks, soups.... You'll find some great ideas here, starting with quesadillas just as good as any you'll find in your favorite Mexican restaurant. There's also a buttery squash soup you'll be proud to serve to grandparents, aunts, uncles, moms, and dads on cool autumn evenings. Happy snacking!

Soups and Starters

Cheesy Bean Quesadilla

These quesadillas make a fun party food or appetizer. Add a side salad and they are a meal in themselves. Sprinkle on a few jalapeno peppers if you want to turn up the heat on this tasty Mexican dish.

Makes 32 pieces

TOOLS

1 baking pan
Waxed paper
1/3 cup dry measuring cup
Large skillet
Spatula
Cutting board
Chef's knife

INGREDIENTS

8 6-inch-wide whole wheat tortillas
2 2/3 cups shredded cheddar cheese, lightly packed
1/2 cup regular salsa or taco sauce
1 cup canned black or kidney beans, drained and rinsed
1/2 cup sour cream

Cheesy Bean Quesadillas

1. Place a baking pan in the oven and preheat to 250°F.

2. Place a tortilla on a large square of waxed paper on the countertop.

3. Lightly pack a 1/3 cup dry measuring cup with cheese. Sprinkle half of the cheese over the bottom half of the tortilla, spreading evenly to within 1/4 inch of the edge.

4. Spoon 1 tablespoon of salsa or taco sauce evenly over the cheese. Spread 2 tablespoons of the beans evenly over the salsa.

5. Sprinkle the remaining half of the cheese over the beans.

6. Fold the top half of the tortilla over the bottom half and press down slightly, but not hard enough to squeeze out any of the ingredients. Set aside.

7. Repeat steps 2 through 6 with the remaining tortillas.

You can make these quesadillas a day ahead of time. Follow steps 2 through 7; then wrap the prepared quesadillas in plastic wrap by pairs. Keep them in the refrigerator until 30 minutes before you plan to cook them.

8. Heat a large skillet over medium heat for about 2 minutes. Carefully place 2 folded quesadillas into the skillet. Press down on the quesadillas with a spatula. Cook until the bottoms of the quesadillas are lightly brown and crisp, about 2 to 3 minutes.

9. Use the spatula to turn the quesadillas and cook on the other side for 2 to 3 minutes. The cheese should be melted.

10. Place the finished quesadillas on the baking pan in the oven to keep warm while you prepare the rest of them.

FUN FACT

In some parts of Mexico, certain fillings for quesadillas are considered a delicious delicacy. These include sautéed squash blossoms and *huitlachoche,* which is basically a large fungus that grows on corn blossoms.

11. When all of the quesadillas are ready, use the spatula to move them one at a time to the cutting board. Slice each into four even triangles by cutting the quesadilla in half first; then cut each half in half again to make four pieces.

12. Serve with a side of sour cream and salsa.

Nutrition Facts per Piece	
Calories	71
Calories from fat	34
Total Fat	4 g
Saturated Fat	2 g
Monounsaturated Fat	1 g
Polyunsaturated Fat	0 g
Cholesterol	10 mg
Sodium	129 mg
Total Carbohydrates	5 g
Dietary Fiber	1 g
Sugars	0 g
Protein	4 g

Red Pepper Pinwheels

These colorful spirals will brighten up any table. They are tangy and chewy with a tiny hint of sweetness.

Makes 48 pieces

TOOLS

Waxed paper
Table knife
Pastry brush
Plastic wrap
Chef's knife

INGREDIENTS

1/2 cup drained roasted red peppers (packed in a jar), patted dry
4 fat-free whole wheat 10-inch tortillas
1/2 cup soft goat cheese or cream cheese at room temperature
4 teaspoons honey Dijon mustard
2 tablespoons chiffonade (thin strips) of fresh basil
4 pinches of pepper

1. Cut the red peppers into 1/4-inch strips and divide into 4 equal portions. Set aside.

2. Place one tortilla on a large square of waxed paper. Use a table knife to spread goat cheese (or cream cheese) evenly over the tortilla. Leave a 1/2 inch cheese-free border around the edge.

3. Use a pastry brush to spread 1 teaspoon of mustard evenly over the cheese. Sprinkle 1/4 of the basil and a pinch of pepper over the cheese.

4. Place half of 1 portion of the red peppers strips in a single line across the center of the tortilla. Place the other half of the portion in a single line about 1 inch from the bottom of the tortilla.

5. Starting at the bottom edge, roll up the tortilla as tightly as possible without poking any holes or ripping it. Tuck the peppers in as you go so that they don't slip out.

6. Roll the tortilla completely to the top edge to make a tube shape. Wrap the rolled tortilla in a sheet of plastic wrap.

7. Repeat steps 2 through 6 with the remaining tortillas. Refrigerate for at least 2 hours or overnight.

8. When you are ready to serve, remove one tortilla from the plastic wrap. Be careful that the tortilla does not unroll.

9. Use a chef's knife to slice off the hollow ends of the tortilla; then cut the rest of it into 12 bite-sized pieces and serve.

> **Tip ● Tip ● Tip**
>
> There are many ways to stuff these pinwheels. Instead of the ingredients listed in this recipe, try sliced salmon strips with cream cheese and basil, sliced turkey strips with cream cheese and cranberry sauce, or sautéed vegetable strips with goat cheese and Ranch dressing.

Nutrition Facts per Piece

Calories	14
Calories from fat	4
Total Fat	0.5 g
Saturated Fat	0.4 g
Monounsaturated Fat	0.1 g
Polyunsaturated Fat	0 g
Cholesterol	1 mg
Sodium	33 mg
Total Carbohydrates	2 g
Dietary Fiber	0 g
Sugars	0 g
Protein	1 g

From the Garden Soup

For a southwestern feast, cook up some steaming bowls of this hearty, garden-fresh soup. Serve it with small bowls of shredded cheddar or Monterey Jack cheese, sour cream, sliced green onions, and crumbled tortilla chips.

Makes 8 servings

TOOLS

1 small bowl
1 large saucepan with a lid
Wooden spoon
Soup ladle

INGREDIENTS

2 garlic cloves, minced
1 tablespoon ground cumin
1/2 teaspoon ground coriander seed
1/2 teaspoon salt and 1/4 teaspoon pepper
2 tablespoons olive oil
1 large onion, diced
4 cups low-sodium vegetable broth
1 can (28 ounces) diced tomatoes
1 can (15 1/2 to 19 ounces) kidney beans, drained and rinsed
2 cups frozen mixed vegetables (do not thaw)

1. In a small bowl, combine the garlic, cumin, coriander, salt, and pepper. Set aside.

2. Add oil to a large saucepan and heat at medium for 1 to 2 minutes.

3. Place the diced onion in the saucepan and stir often until it is softened, about 5 minutes.

4. Add the garlic and seasoning mixture to the onion. Stir continuously for 1 minute.

5. Add the tomatoes and vegetable broth to the saucepan. Stir well. Increase the heat to bring the soup to a boil.

6. Once it is boiling, stir in the kidney beans and frozen vegetables. Bring to a boil again.

To make your soup even heartier, add a cup of cooked rice or pasta before serving.

7. Reduce the heat until the soup simmers; then cover the pan with the lid. Let the mixture simmer for about 10 minutes, stirring occasionally.

8. Remove the saucepan from the heat and use a ladle to serve the soup into bowls.

FUN FACT
Currently, the largest "bowl" of vegetable soup ever made measured more than 1,000 gallons. It was prepared in Poland by 8 chefs and included more than 250 pounds of vegetables.

Nutrition Facts per Serving

Calories	177
Calories from fat	42
Total Fat	5 g
Saturated Fat	1 g
Monounsaturated Fat	3 g
Polyunsaturated Fat	0 g
Cholesterol	0 mg
Sodium	535 mg
Total Carbohydrates	26 g
Dietary Fiber	7 g
Sugars	6 g
Protein	9 g

Buttery Butternut Soup

When autumn arrives, the markets are filled with colorful squash and pumpkins. It is a perfect time to prepare this rich butternut soup as a first course to a meal. Like many homemade soups, it tastes even better the day after it is made.

Makes 8 servings

TOOLS

1 large stockpot with a lid
Large bowl
Wooden spoon
Soup ladle
Blender

INGREDIENTS

2 tablespoons olive oil
2 medium onions, diced
3 medium carrots, chopped
2 celery stalks, chopped
1/4 teaspoon ground nutmeg
1/4 teaspoon dried thyme leaves
6 cups low-sodium vegetable broth
1 can (14 ounces) pure pumpkin, unsweetened
2 teaspoons salt and 1/4 teaspoon pepper
2 1/2 pounds roasted butternut squash
pieces (Cut squash in half, roast for about
1/2 hour. Then scoop out insides.)

1. Add the oil to the stockpot and heat over medium heat for 1 to 2 minutes.

2. Place the onions in the stockpot and stir often until softened, about 5 minutes.

3. Add the carrots and celery to the stockpot and cook, stirring often, for about 5 minutes.

4. Add the nutmeg and thyme to the stockpot and stir to combine.

5. Add the vegetable broth, pumpkin, salt, pepper, and roasted squash to the stockpot. Stir well to combine. Increase the heat to bring the mixture to a boil.

6. Reduce the heat so that the soup will simmer; then cover the pot with a lid. Stir occasionally until the vegetables are tender, about 30 minutes.

7. Use a heat-proof soup ladle to transfer the soup in small batches to the blender. Puree until smooth. Pour into a large bowl and set aside. You may substitute a handheld immersion blender instead of a standing blender. The immersion blender will save time because it can puree the soup right in the stockpot.

8. Repeat step 7 until all of the soup has been pureed. Return the soup in the bowl to the stockpot. Simmer uncovered for about 10 minutes until the flavors have blended and the soup is hot. Ladle into small bowls and serve with a sprinkling of nutmeg on the top.

> Be sure to remove the lid of the blender carefully. Steam can build up inside the blender and cause burns when you remove the lid. Puree in small batches so the soup doesn't spray out when you remove the lid.

Nutrition Facts per Serving	
Calories	181
Calories from fat	45
Total Fat	5 g
Saturated Fat	1 g
Monounsaturated Fat	3 g
Polyunsaturated Fat	1 g
Cholesterol	0 mg
Sodium	665 mg
Total Carbohydrates	32 g
Dietary Fiber	5 g
Sugars	8 g
Protein	7 g

CHAPTER 7

When someone asks what you had for dinner, you might respond, "chicken," or "spaghetti," but that's usually only a part of what was on your plate. Salads and side dishes give you a chance to create some colorful and tasty dishes to accompany the meat or pasta that is the main dish; they're also a source of vitamins and nutrients that your body needs. And, mostly, they really taste good and give dinner some extra eye and taste appeal.

Salads and Sides

Dress It Up Dressings

Every salad needs a dressing, and home-made from fresh ingredients is much better than bottled. Here are four that will add sparkle to your greens.

Fat-Free Tomato Dressing

A garden salad with this tangy dressing will wake up your taste buds. If you store the dressing in a sealed container in the refrigerator it will last for about a week. It also works well as a marinade for chicken, beef, or pork.

Makes about 2/3 cup of dressing

TOOLS

Small bowl
Whisk

INGREDIENTS

1/2 cup tomato juice
1 tablespoon balsamic vinegar
1/2 teaspoon Dijon mustard
2 garlic cloves, minced
1/4 teaspoon salt and 1/8 teaspoon pepper
1/8 teaspoon hot sauce (optional)
1/8 teaspoon dried oregano leaves or
   Italian seasoning

1. In a small bowl, whisk the ingredients together until well blended.

Add 1 tablespoon of mayonnaise to make a creamy tomato dressing. It will no longer be fat-free, but you can also use light or fat-free mayo if you want.

Asian Style Dressing

This sweet and sour dressing is perfect for a Chinese chicken salad, or use it to spice up a salad made with shredded cabbage and diced pineapple. You might even try it warm over an omelet stuffed with shrimp and green onion.

Makes about 1 cup of dressing

Citrus Dressing

The orange flavor of this dressing makes it a perfect match for delicate greens such as butter leaf lettuce or spinach. It is also excellent served warm over steamed green beans or drizzled over poached salmon. Its citrus flavor makes it a perfect marinade for fish and seafood.

Makes about 2/3 cup

Indian Dressing

This low-fat dressing's creamy flavor is tasty over salads that include spicy greens such as mustard greens or arugula. As a marinade, it compliments the delicate flavor of chicken or fish.

Makes about 1 1/4 cups

TOOLS

Small bowl
Whisk

INGREDIENTS

2 garlic cloves, minced
1 green onion, minced
1/4 cup rice vinegar
3 tablespoons toasted sesame oil
2 tablespoons hoisin sauce

2 tablespoons granulated sugar
1/4 teaspoon chili paste
1/2 teaspoon ground ginger

1. In a small bowl, whisk the ingredients together until well blended.

Add peanut flavor to the dressing by stirring in 1/4 cup of creamy peanut butter.

TOOLS

Small bowl
Whisk

INGREDIENTS

1 tablespoon Dijon mustard
2 tablespoons balsamic vinegar
1/8 teaspoon salt and 1/8 teaspoon pepper
1/3 cup extra virgin olive oil
3 tablespoons orange juice
1 teaspoon liquid honey

1. In a small bowl, add the Dijon mustard, vinegar, salt, and pepper. Whisk well.

2. Slowly add the oil, and whisk for 1 minute.

3. Whisk in the orange juice and honey until blended.

Try substituting lime or grapefruit juice for the orange juice in this recipe.

TOOLS

Small skillet
Small bowl
Whisk

INGREDIENTS

1 tablespoon ground coriander seed
1 1/2 teaspoons ground cumin
3 garlic cloves, minced
1 tablespoon freshly grated ginger root
1 teaspoon salt
1/2 teaspoon turmeric
1/4 teaspoon ground cayenne pepper
1 cup plain nonfat yogurt
2 tablespoons fresh lemon juice

1. Place coriander and cumin in a small skillet. Heat and stir for about 1 minute.

2. Pour the mixture into a small bowl and add the rest of the ingredients. Whisk together until well blended.

If you have a little of this dressing left over, boil some eggs and halve them as if you were making devilled eggs. Use 2 tablespoons of Indian Dressing in the yolk mixture. You can also spread it on a slice of bread and broil it for a minute or two in the oven.

Summery Spinach Salad

Why make the same old salad when you can serve this healthy option? With the nutty crunch of pine nuts and the sweet juicy tang of mandarin oranges, you can serve this dish with pride.

Makes 4 servings

TOOLS

Small skillet
Wooden spoon
Large, wide salad bowl
Small mixing bowl
Whisk
Salad tongs

INGREDIENTS

1/3 cup pine nuts
8 cups (6 ounce bag) baby spinach
1/2 small red onion, halved lengthwise and thinly sliced
1/2 cup drained canned mandarin orange segments, patted dry
1/4 cup plain, low-fat yogurt
1 teaspoon Dijon mustard
2 tablespoons balsamic vinegar
1 pinch salt and 1 pinch pepper

1. Place the pine nuts in a small skillet over medium heat for 1 to 2 minutes until they are lightly browned.

2. Move the pine nuts to a small plate to cool and set aside.

3. Place the spinach leaves in a large salad bowl. Layer the onion slices on top of the spinach and the orange slices in the center.

4. In a small bowl, mix the yogurt, Dijon mustard, vinegar, salt, and pepper.

5. Using the whisk, thoroughly blend the ingredients to create the salad dressing.

6. Before serving the salad, pour on the dressing and toss the ingredients with the salad tongs. Sprinkle on the toasted pine nuts and serve.

You can vary the fruit and nuts in the salad. Try substituting slivered almonds, pecans, or walnuts for the pine nuts. Instead of oranges, use dried cranberries, cherries, or slivered dried apricots. Toss in 4 ounces of blue cheese or goat cheese if you like.

FUN FACT

Pine nuts are harvested from the Stone Pine. The cone of the Stone Pine takes three years to mature and release its seeds.

Nutrition Facts per Serving

Calories	119
Calories from fat	72
Total Fat	.8 g
Saturated Fat	1 g
Monounsaturated Fat	2 g
Polyunsaturated Fat	4 g
Cholesterol	1 mg
Sodium	67 mg
Total Carbohydrates	9 g
Dietary Fiber	2 g
Sugars	4 g
Protein	4 g

Classic Caesar Salad

The original Caesar salad was invented in a restaurant in Tijuana, Mexico. It became so popular that movie stars and other famous people of the time would travel many miles to enjoy one. You can make one of these award-winning salads in your own kitchen.

Makes 4 servings

TOOLS

Large salad bowl
Small mixing bowls
Whisk
Salad tongs

You can turn this salad into a main dish by adding grilled chicken breast, strips of steak, or sautéed shrimp.

INGREDIENTS

8 cups of romaine lettuce, cleaned and torn into bite-sized pieces
2 cloves garlic, minced
2 tablespoons fresh lemon juice
1 tablespoon Dijon mustard
1/4 teaspoon salt
1/4 teaspoon pepper
1/2 teaspoon Worcestershire sauce
1/4 cup extra virgin olive oil
4 tablespoons freshly grated parmesan cheese
1 cup croutons

1. Place the romaine lettuce in a large salad bowl.

2. In a small mixing bowl, combine the garlic, lemon juice, Dijon mustard, salt, pepper, and Worcestershire sauce. Stir with a whisk until well blended.

3. Slowly pour the olive oil into the bowl, whisking continuously until the olive oil is blended well into the mixture.

4. Stir in 1 tablespoon of the grated parmesan cheese.

5. Just before serving, pour the dressing over the lettuce in the salad bowl. Add the croutons and toss everything well with the salad tongs.

6. Sprinkle the remaining parmesan cheese on the salad and serve.

FUN FACT

The Caesar salad was originally served with the lettuce leaves in a circle on a flat plate. The stems faced out so that the salad could be picked up and eaten with the fingers.

Nutrition Facts per Serving	
Calories	213
Calories from fat	51
Total Fat	17 g
Saturated Fat	3 g
Monounsaturated Fat	11 g
Polyunsaturated Fat	1 g
Cholesterol	8 mg
Sodium	354 mg
Total Carbohydrates	10 g
Dietary Fiber	1 g
Sugars	2 g
Protein	6 g

Confetti Potato Salad

This potato salad is a people pleaser whether it is presented at the dinner table or at the next family picnic. You can serve it warm or chilled.

Makes 4 servings

TOOLS

Large saucepan
Paring knife
Large mixing bowl
Whisk
Colander
Chef's knife
Large serving bowl
Salad tongs

INGREDIENTS

1 1/2 pounds small new potatoes, scrubbed
2 tablespoons sherry vinegar
2 tablespoons olive oil
1/2 teaspoon salt and 1/4 teaspoon pepper
1 red pepper, diced
1 stalk celery, diced
2 green onions in 1/4-inch slices

1. Place the potatoes in a large saucepan and cover with about 1 inch of water. Put the pan on high heat and bring the water to a boil.

2. Continue to cook the potatoes until they are tender when pierced with a fork, about 15 to 20 minutes.

3. Drain the potatoes into a large colander in the sink.

4. Combine the vinegar, oil, salt, and pepper in large mixing bowl. Stir with a whisk until blended. Add the red pepper, celery, and green onions to the mixture. Stir well.

5. Use a chef's knife to slice each potato into 4 pieces. If the potatoes are still warm, hold them with a paper towel. Put all of the cut potatoes in the large mixing bowl.

6. Using salad tongs, toss the ingredients so that the potatoes absorb the liquid. Serve warm or chilled.

> To make a creamy potato salad, add 2 tablespoons of mayonnaise at step 4. If you want some meat in the salad, try 1/2 cup of chopped smoked salmon or ham.

Nutrition Facts per Serving

Calories	225
Calories from fat	78
Total Fat	9 g
Saturated Fat	1 g
Monounsaturated Fat	6 g
Polyunsaturated Fat	2 g
Cholesterol	2 mg
Sodium	361 mg
Total Carbohydrates	34 g
Dietary Fiber	5 g
Sugars	3 g
Protein	4 g

Mouth-Watering Mushrooms

Mushrooms have a unique flavor that complements many other dishes. This side dish can be a delicious partner to a roast or sautéed chicken breast.

Makes 4 servings

TOOLS

Small mixing bowl
Spoon
Large skillet
Wooden spoon

INGREDIENTS

2 cloves of garlic, minced
1/2 teaspoon salt and 1/8 teaspoon pepper
2 tablespoons olive oil
1 pound fresh white or brown mushrooms, sliced
1 tablespoon balsamic vinegar
2 tablespoons finely chopped parsley

1. In a small bowl, combine the garlic, salt, and pepper. Set aside.

2. Heat the oil in a large skillet at medium-high heat for about 1 minute. Add the mushrooms to the pan. Use a wooden spoon to turn them and coat them with oil.

3. Cook the mushrooms, stirring occasionally, until they are cooked through and lightly browned, about 5 minutes.

FUN FACT
Mushrooms contain 80% to 90% water. They are also very low in calories. The ancient Greeks believed that mushrooms provided great strength for warriors in battle.

Try using different herbs, such as basil or cilantro, in this dish. If you choose strong-flavored herbs such as rosemary or tarragon, use only 1 tablespoon.

4. Add the garlic mixture to the pan and stir for 1 minute more.

5. Add the balsamic vinegar and stir. Turn off the heat and stir in the parsley. Serve immediately.

Nutrition Facts per Serving	
Calories	91
Calories from fat	65
Total Fat	7g
Saturated Fat	1g
Monounsaturated Fat	5g
Polyunsaturated Fat	1g
Cholesterol	0 mg
Sodium	299 mg
Total Carbohydrates	5 g
Dietary Fiber	0 g
Sugars	3 g
Protein	2 g

Classic Rice Pilaf

Rice pilaf is a classic side dish. It can be served with barbecued ribs or chicken, and it's great with fish.

Makes 4 servings

TOOLS

Large saucepan with lid (make sure both saucepan and lid are ovenproof)
Wooden spoon

This dish can be prepared with a variety of ingredients. When you add the broth, try adding 2 tablespoons of toasted pine nuts, 1 peeled, seeded, and chopped tomato, or 1/3 cup toasted almonds.

INGREDIENTS

2 tablespoons olive oil
1/2 small onion, minced
1 cup long-grain brown rice or brown basmati rice
2 cups low sodium chicken or vegetable broth
1/2 teaspoon dried thyme leaves
1/2 teaspoon turmeric
1/2 teaspoon pepper
1 bay leaf

1. Preheat the oven to 350°F.
2. Add the oil to a large saucepan and heat for about 1 minute. Add the onion and cook, stirring occasionally for 1 minute more.

3. Add the rice to the saucepan, and stir to coat it with oil and onion. Stir for about 2 minutes.

4. Pour the broth into the saucepan. Be careful because the broth may splatter or steam.

5. Stir the broth as you add in the thyme, turmeric, pepper, and bay leaf. Increase the heat to a boil. Cover the saucepan and place it in the oven. Cook until the rice has absorbed the liquid, about 45 to 50 minutes.

6. Using oven mitts, remove the saucepan and let the rice sit, covered, for about 10 minutes.

7. Remove the lid and take the bay leaf out of the rice and discard. Fluff the rice with a fork and serve.

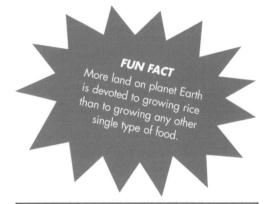

FUN FACT
More land on planet Earth is devoted to growing rice than to growing any other single type of food.

Nutrition Facts per Serving	
Calories	259
Calories from fat	82
Total Fat	9 g
Saturated Fat	1 g
Monounsaturated Fat	6 g
Polyunsaturated Fat	1 g
Cholesterol	0 mg
Sodium	40 mg
Total Carbohydrates	39 g
Dietary Fiber	2 g
Sugars	1 g
Protein	6 g

Mashed Potatoes

Few people can resist a buttery serving of mashed potatoes. The secret ingredient in this recipe for yummy mashed potatoes is buttermilk.

Makes 6 servings

TOOLS

Large saucepan
Paring knife
Large colander
Potato masher

INGREDIENTS

3 large Yukon Gold potatoes, cut into
    1 1/2-inch chunks
1/2 cup buttermilk (shake the carton well
    before pouring)
2/3 cup 1% milk
1 tablespoon unsalted butter
1 teaspoon salt and 1/8 teaspoon pepper

1. Place the potato chunks in a large saucepan and add cold water to cover the potatoes by about 1 inch. Heat the saucepan over high heat until the water comes to a boil. Add 1 tablespoon of salt.

2. Continue to boil the potatoes until they are tender when pierced with a paring knife (about 15 minutes). Drain the potatoes in a large colander in the sink.

3. Return the potatoes to the empty saucepan. Place the saucepan on a cold burner on the stove. Add the milk, buttermilk, and butter. Use the potato masher to mash the potatoes to the texture you prefer.

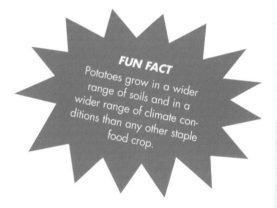

Monitor the potatoes carefully when they are boiling. Adjust the burner temperature to make sure the water does not boil over.

4. Add the salt and pepper and stir with a wooden spoon to blend all of the ingredients.

If you want the potatoes to be creamier, add a little more milk.

FUN FACT
Potatoes grow in a wider range of soils and in a wider range of climate conditions than any other staple food crop.

Nutrition Facts per Serving	
Calories	180
Calories from fat	22
Total Fat	2 g
Saturated Fat	2 g
Monounsaturated Fat	0 g
Polyunsaturated Fat	0 g
Cholesterol	8 mg
Sodium	436 mg
Total Carbohydrates	35 g
Dietary Fiber	4 g
Sugars	4 g
Protein	5 g

Roasted Vegetables

This side dish is a sweet treat. Carrots, parsnips, and sweet potatoes contain sugars that are given a flavor boost by roasting.

Makes 4 servings

TOOLS

9 ×13 baking sheet
Parchment paper
Large bowl
Serving spatula

INGREDIENTS

1/2 pound each carrots, parsnips, and sweet potatoes, scrubbed and cut into 1-inch chunks
2 tablespoons olive oil
1/4 teaspoon dried thyme
1 teaspoon salt

1. Preheat the oven to 425°F.

2. Cover the bottom of a 9 ×13 baking sheet with parchment paper.

3. Place the parsnips, carrots, and sweet potatoes in a large bowl. Add the oil, thyme, and salt to the bowl. Use your hands to mix the vegetables to be sure they are coated well with oil.

4. Place the vegetables in a single layer on the prepared baking sheet. Place the baking sheet in the oven for 35 to 40 minutes.

5. Roast until the vegetables are tender but still slightly firm when pierced with a paring knife. Remove the baking sheet from the oven.

6. Using a spatula, place the vegetables into a serving platter or bowl.

FUN FACT
Parsnips are related to carrots and celery. They can be prepared in a variety of ways including deep fried as chips. In Ireland, they are used to make beer and wine.

Nutrition Facts per Serving	
Calories	177
Calories from fat	66
Total Fat	7 g
Saturated Fat	1 g
Monounsaturated Fat	5 g
Polyunsaturated Fat	1 g
Cholesterol	0 mg
Sodium	634 mg
Total Carbohydrates	7 g
Dietary Fiber	6 g
Sugars	9 g
Protein	2 g

Turn roasted vegetables into a flavorsome party dip by placing 1 cup of vegetables and 4 ounces of cream cheese in a food processor. Blend well and serve with tortilla chips.

Roasty Toasty Potato Wedges

These golden brown potato wedges are so good they might not make it from the baking pan to the serving dish.

Makes 4 servings

TOOLS

9 ×13 baking sheet
Parchment paper
Chef's knife
Small mixing bowl
Whisk
Large mixing bowl

INGREDIENTS

4 large russet potatoes
2 teaspoons garlic powder
1 teaspoon paprika
1 teaspoon dry mustard
1 teaspoon salt and 1/4 teaspoon pepper
1/2 teaspoon dried thyme leaves
1/4 teaspoon sugar
1/4 cup water
2 tablespoons olive oil

1. Preheat the oven to 425°F.

2. Cover the bottom of a 9 ×13 baking sheet with parchment paper.

3. To cut a potato into wedges, cut the potato in half using a chef's knife. Place each half of the potato cut side down.

4. Cut each half of the potato lengthwise to create 4 wedges. Cut each potato wedge lengthwise to create 8 wedges.

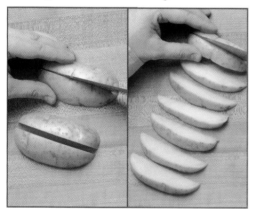

5. Repeat steps 3 and 4 with the remaining potatoes. You will have 32 wedges.

6. In a small bowl, use a whisk to mix together the garlic powder, paprika, dry mustard, salt, pepper, thyme, and sugar. Add the oil and whisk thoroughly.

7. Place the potato wedges in a large bowl. Pour 1/4 cup of water over them.

8. Pour the oil and seasoning mixture over the potatoes. With your hands, toss the potato wedges to be sure they are well coated with oil and seasoning.

9. Place the potato wedges in a single layer on the prepared baking sheet and drizzle any remaining oil and seasoning over them. Bake until the potatoes are tender and golden brown, about 35 to 40 minutes.

10. Remove from the oven and serve immediately.

Nutrition Facts per Serving	
Calories	358
Calories from fat	68
Total Fat	8
Saturated Fat	1 g
Monounsaturated Fat	5 g
Polyunsaturated Fat	1 g
Cholesterol	0 mg
Sodium	646 mg
Total Carbohydrates	67 g
Dietary Fiber	9 g
Sugars	4 g
Protein	8 g

CHAPTER 8

Be a good egg. Use your noodle. Eggs and noodles are so much a part of our lives that we've used them to describe being a likable person and exercising your brain. Eggs and noodles are the original comfort foods. Scrambled or fried eggs with toast and bacon are thought of as the all-American breakfast; noodles, pasta, and macaroni are some of the first foods we come to love when we begin to learn to feed ourselves.

Eggs and Noodles

Sunny-Side Up Eggs

Sunny-side up, or fried, eggs shouldn't be too hard or too runny. The trick is to get the yolks cooked properly without overcooking the whites. With a little practice, you will be able to cook them perfectly every time.

Makes 1 serving.

©istockphoto.com/Denis Kotov

TOOLS

Large skillet with lid
2 small bowls
Wide spatula

INGREDIENTS

2 eggs
1 tablespoon butter
1 tablespoon olive oil

1. Break both eggs, each into its own small bowl. Be careful not to break the yolks.

2. Add the oil and butter to a large skillet and heat over medium-low for about a minute. Pick up the pan by the handle and swirl the contents gently until the butter is melted and combined with the olive oil. Set the pan down again on the burner.

3. Hold one of the small bowls low over the skillet toward one side of the pan. Carefully tip the egg into the hot oil. Repeat with the second egg but to the other side of the pan. The whites will begin to cook immediately. The eggs should be side-by-side but not touching.

4. Cover with a lid and allow the eggs to cook for about 2 minutes.

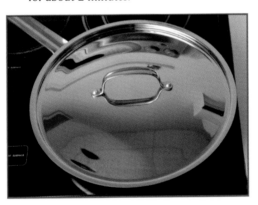

5. Remove the lid and set it aside. Gently touch one yolk with your fingertip to test for doneness. It should be firm and no longer cold. The egg whites should be solid. If the eggs are not done, cover the pan with the lid and cook for another 30 seconds.

6. When the yolks are done the way you like them, remove the skillet to a cool burner. Use a wide spatula to lift each egg and place it on a plate.

Nutrition Facts per Egg	
Calories	90
Calories from fat	63
Total Fat	7 g
Saturated Fat	2 g
Cholesterol	210 mg
Sodium	94 mg
Total Carbohydrates	0 g
Dietary Fiber	0 g
Sugars	0 g
Protein	6 g

Tip • Tip • Tip • Tip • Tip • Tip • Tip • Tip

Some people prefer their eggs once-over, or over-easy. That means that once the eggs are cooked on one side, they are flipped over and cooked a while longer. To prepare once-over eggs follow steps 1 through 4 in the recipe. Using a wide spatula, carefully flip each egg over and cook yolk-side-down for about 30 seconds and then serve.

Scrambled Eggs

Scrambled eggs are easy to make, and they can be dished up in many ways. Serve them plain or with shredded cheese, chopped herbs, sour cream, salsa, or bacon crumbles on top.

Makes 1 serving

TOOLS

Medium bowl
Whisk
Large skillet
Flat-edged wooden spoon

INGREDIENTS

2 eggs per serving
1 tablespoon milk for every two eggs
1 tablespoon butter

1. Break two eggs for each serving into a medium bowl. Add 1 tablespoon of milk per serving.

2. Tilt the bowl toward you and use a whisk to beat the eggs in a circular motion until the milk is blended in. Do not over-beat.

3. Add 1 tablespoon of butter to the skillet and heat over medium heat for about 1 minute. Then pick up the pan by the handle and swirl the butter gently until it is completely melted.

4. Pour the egg mixture into the skillet and allow it to cook for 30 seconds. Using the wooden spoon, stir the eggs by pushing them toward the center of the pan. (You could also use a flat-edged wooden spatula.) This will create small lumps, or curds. Continue to stir until the eggs are only slightly runny.

5. Remove the pan from the heat and continue to stir the eggs until they are cooked through. Serve immediately.

FUN FACT

In the United States, chickens may produce more than 72 billion eggs a day. The most popular egg-laying chickens are White Leghorns. Many of these modern chickens are descendants of chickens brought to America by Christopher Columbus from the Italian city of Livorno.

You don't have to serve scrambled eggs on a plate. You can spoon the cooked eggs into a pita bread pocket, serve them between two toasted English muffins, or wrap them in a warm tortilla.

Nutrition Facts per 1/2 Cup Serving	
Calories	178
Calories from fat	108
Total Fat	12 g
Saturated Fat	4 g
Monounsaturated Fat	4.5 g
Polyunsaturated Fat	1.5 g
Cholesterol	514 mg
Sodium	170 mg
Total Carbohydrates	1 g
Sugars	1 g
Protein	15 g

Veggie Cheese Omelet

A light, fluffy omelet is a great choice for breakfast, lunch, or even dinner! This recipe uses 2 eggs per omelet, but you can use 3 eggs if you like. For the best omelets, before starting to cook, place the fresh eggs with the shell on into a large bowl and add hot tap water to cover the eggs. Wait four minutes; then use a spoon to remove the eggs.

Makes 2 omelets

TOOLS

1 large skillet
1 small skillet
Flat-edged wooden mixing spoon
2 small mixing bowls
Fork or whisk
Heat-proof rubber spatula

INGREDIENTS

1 tablespoon extra virgin olive oil
1/2 small onion, halved and thinly sliced
1 cup frozen mixed vegetables (thawed) Or use fresh chopped tomatoes, onions, broccoli, or asparagus).
1/8 teaspoon dried oregano leaves
1/8 teaspoon each of salt and pepper
4 eggs
2 tablespoons butter
1/4 cup grated cheddar or Swiss cheese

1. Warm a large skillet over medium heat for about 1 to 2 minutes.

2. Add the oil to the skillet and heat for about 30 seconds.

3. Place the onion in the skillet and stir often until it is softened, about 5 minutes.

4. Add the vegetables, oregano, salt, and pepper. Cook until the vegetables are heated through, about 2 to 5 minutes. Place the vegetables in a bowl and set aside.

FUN FACT
The record for making omelets was set by Howard Helmer when he served up 427 in 30 minutes!

5. Break 2 eggs into a small bowl. Lightly beat the eggs with a fork or a whisk.

6. Heat a small skillet over medium-low heat for about 1 to 2 minutes.

7. Add 1 tablespoon of butter to the skillet and swirl the skillet slowly to coat its surface.

8. Add the beaten eggs to the skillet. Allow the eggs to sit in the skillet until the bottom becomes solid, about 1 minute.

9. Slip a heat-proof rubber spatula under one edge of the eggs, gently pushing toward the center of the skillet. Some of the wet egg will run into the pan.

10. Repeat step 9, moving the spatula to the right each time. After 2 or 3 minutes you should have completed a circle of the pan and little or no wet egg should be left on the surface. Remove the skillet from the burner.

11. Spoon half of the cheese and half of the vegetable mixture evenly onto one half of the omelet. Use a heatproof rubber spatula to fold the other half of the omelet over the filling.

12. Using the spatula, carefully slide the omelet onto a plate and serve. Repeat steps 5–12 with the remaining ingredients to make another serving.

Use your imagination to create fillings for omelets or try some of these ideas:

- 2/3 cup sautéed mushrooms and 1/4 cup grated Swiss cheese.

- 2/3 cup smoked salmon, 2 tablespoons chopped green onions, and 1/4 cup crumbled soft goat cheese.

- 1/2 cup diced ham, 1/2 cup diced cooked potatoes or bell pepper, and 1/4 cup grated cheddar cheese.

Nutrition Facts per Omelet	
Calories	395
Calories from fat	284
Total Fat	32 g
Saturated Fat	14 g
Monounsaturated Fat	13 g
Polyunsaturated Fat	2 g
Cholesterol	416 mg
Sodium	453 mg
Total Carbohydrates	10 g
Dietary Fiber	3 g
Sugars	4 g
Protein	16 g

Fettuccine Alfredo

Made with butter, cheese, cream, and thin ribbons of pasta, Fettuccine Alfredo is rich, smooth, and satisfying.

Makes 6 servings

TOOLS

Covered stockpot
Large sauté pan
Glass liquid measuring cup
Large colander
2 wooden spoons

INGREDIENTS

2 tablespoons extra virgin olive oil
1/2 small onion, minced
1 cup heavy cream
1/4 teaspoon pepper
1/2 cup (1 stick) unsalted butter, cut into 1/2-inch cubes
12 ounces egg fettuccine
1 cup fresh Parmigiano Reggiano cheese, finely grated
2 tablespoons finely chopped parsley

1. Fill a stockpot 2/3 full with cold water. Bring the water to a boil; then decrease the heat so that the water continues to bubble gently. Put a lid on the stockpot.

2. Add the olive oil to a large sauté pan and heat over medium for about 1 minute. Add the mined onion and stir with a wooden spoon for 1 minute.

Stockpot

Sauté pan

3. Add the cream to the pan and stir. Toss in the butter and pepper. Stir until the butter melts.

4. Increase the heat to medium-high and allow to cook for 1 minute, stirring occasionally. Turn off the heat.

5. Add 1 tablespoon of salt to the stockpot and bring the water back to a boil. Add the pasta. Stir and separate the long strands for about 1 minute. Boil the pasta until it is barely al dente, about 5 minutes. Turn off the heat.

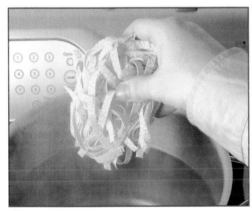

6. Use a glass measuring cup to scoop about 2/3 cup of hot water from the stockpot and set aside.

7. Drain the pasta into a colander in the sink. Do not shake off the excess water and do not rinse.

8. Add the pasta and 1/3 cup of the reserved cooking water to the cream sauce in the sauté pan. Turn the heat to medium high.

9. Use two wooden spoons to toss the pasta with the sauce until the pasta is well coated, about 1 minute. Turn off the heat, add 1 cup of grated cheese and the parsley, and then toss again.

10. Serve piping hot with a sprinkle of chopped parsley and some grated cheese on top.

Nutrition Facts per Serving	
Calories	613
Calories from fat	375
Total Fat	42 g
Saturated Fat	23 g
Monounsaturated Fat	14 g
Polyunsaturated Fat	2 g
Cholesterol	161 mg
Sodium	73 mg
Total Carbohydrates	44 g
Dietary Fiber	2 g
Sugars	2 g
Protein	16 g

Spinach-Stuffed Pasta Shells

You'll love this cheesy pasta dish. The stuffed shells make a pretty presentation, and they go well with a variety of sauces. They keep well in the refrigerator and may be made a day ahead of time.

Makes 6 servings

TOOLS

9 ×13-inch baking pan
Stockpot
Slotted spoon
Colander
Dinner plate
Large bowl
Small bowl
Wooden spoon
Tablespoon
Aluminum foil

INGREDIENTS

1/2 pound jumbo pasta shells, about 30 shells
1 package (10 ounces) frozen chopped spinach, cooked and drained
1 jar (26 ounces) pasta sauce
16 ounces part-skim ricotta cheese
2 cups shredded mozzarella cheese
1/2 teaspoon ground nutmeg
1 teaspoon salt and 1/4 teaspoon pepper
2 eggs

1. Preheat the oven to 350°F and lightly coat the inside of a 9 ×13-inch baking pan with oil.

2. In a stockpot, cook the pasta shells according to package directions until they are done. Using a slotted spoon, remove the shells and place them in a colander in the sink and rinse with cold water. Set aside.

In step 2, to test the pasta shells to see if they are done, use a slotted spoon to take one shell out of the boiling water. Run the shell under cold tap water and open it with your fingers. If it opens easily, it is ready. If it starts to tear, put it back in the pot and cook for another minute. Keep checking until the shells are done.

4. In a large bowl, combine the spinach, ricotta cheese, 1 cup shredded mozzarella, nutmeg, salt, and pepper.

3. With your hands, squeeze any excess moisture out of the spinach and set it aside.

Spread 1 1/4 cups of pasta sauce over the bottom of the oiled baking pan. Set aside.

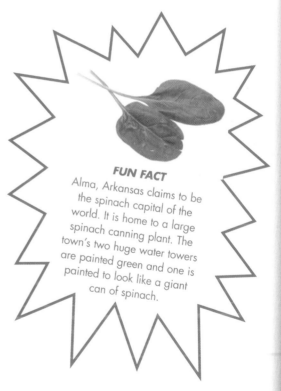

FUN FACT

Alma, Arkansas claims to be the spinach capital of the world. It is home to a large spinach canning plant. The town's two huge water towers are painted green and one is painted to look like a giant can of spinach.

5. Break the eggs into a small bowl, and then add them to the spinach mixture. With a wooden spoon, stir well to combine the ingredients.

6. Set the colander with the drained pasta shells on a plate on the countertop. Holding a pasta shell open with one hand, spoon 1 heaping tablespoon of spinach filling into the shell. Place the shell open side up on the sauce in the baking pan. Fill each of the shells and place them in the pan side-by-side in about three rows.

7. Once the pan is filled with stuffed shells, slowly pour the rest of the pasta sauce evenly over the shells. Sprinkle the second cup of mozzarella cheese evenly over the entire dish.

8. Cover the pan loosely with foil and bake in the center rack of the oven until the sauce is bubbling gently, about 20 to 25 minutes. Remove the aluminum foil but leave the pan in the oven.

9. Continue to bake until the cheese is melted and the sauce is bubbling quickly, about 10 to 15 minutes.

10. Remove the pan and allow it to sit for 2 minutes before serving.

Nutrition Facts per Serving

Calories	451
Calories from fat	173
Total Fat	19 g
Saturated Fat	11 g
Monounsaturated Fat	5 g
Polyunsaturated Fat	1 g
Cholesterol	120 mg
Sodium	1419 mg
Total Carbohydrates	44 g
Dietary Fiber	5 g
Sugars	8 g
Protein	28 g

On Top of Spaghetti

Ask anyone what his or her top 10 favorite dishes are and spaghetti will probably be on the list. Serve them this spaghetti and meat sauce made from scratch, and spaghetti may make it to the top of the list.

Makes 6 servings

TOOLS

Large sauté pan with lid
2 wooden spoons
Stockpot
Colander

INGREDIENTS

1 tablespoon extra virgin olive oil
2 pounds lean ground beef or turkey

2 medium onions, diced
3 cloves garlic, minced
1 can (5 1/2 ounces) tomato paste, plus
    1 can water
1 can (28 ounces) whole tomatoes
1 tablespoon dried Italian seasoning
2 teaspoons salt and 1/2 teaspoon pepper
2 bay leaves
1 1/2 pounds spaghetti

1. Fill a stockpot 2/3 full with cold water. Bring the water to a boil, and then decrease the heat so that the water continues to bubble gently. Put a lid on the stockpot.

2. Add the olive oil to a large sauté pan and heat over medium-high heat for about 1 minute. Add the ground meat to the pan. Cook the meat, breaking it up with the edge of a wooden spoon. Stir occasionally until there is no more pink showing in the meat, about 8 to 10 minutes.

3. Reduce the heat to medium and add the diced onions to the meat. Use a clean wooden spoon to stir until the onions are softened, about 5 minutes.

4. Add the garlic, tomato paste, can of water, and whole tomatoes. Break up the tomatoes with the edge of the spoon.

5. Add the Italian seasoning, salt, pepper, and bay leaves. Stir until the mixture is combined and the sauce is bubbling briskly.

FUN FACT

According to a recent study, the favorite family meal in the United States is spaghetti. It is followed by grilled chicken and pizza.

You can create a vegetarian version of this pasta sauce. Follow steps 3 through 6 but simmer for only 30 minutes. Add 2 packages (24 ounces) of soy-based ground meat substitute. Stir and let cook for 10 minutes more; then continue with steps 7 and 8.

6. Reduce the heat to simmer and allow the sauce to bubble gently. Partially cover the sauté pan with a lid; you want to leave a small opening so that the steam can escape. Simmer until the meat is tender and most of the liquid has been absorbed, about 40 minutes. Stir occasionally to prevent sticking.

7. Turn off the heat. Remove the lid and let the sauce rest for about 10 minutes. Remove the bay leaves.

8. In the stockpot, cook the pasta according to package directions until it is done. Drain the pasta in the colander in the sink. Do not rinse. Serve the pasta and top it generously with meat sauce.

Nutrition Facts per Serving	
Calories	822
Calories from fat	225
Total Fat	25g
Saturated Fat	9 g
Monounsaturated Fat	11 g
Polyunsaturated Fat	2 g
Cholesterol	90 mg
Sodium	1066 mg
Total Carbohydrates	99 g
Dietary Fiber	6 g
Sugars	9 g
Protein	47 g

CHAPTER 9

Beef and pork contain streaks of fat, called *marbling*, which run through each cut of meat. Marbling adds taste, but extra lean beef and pork still have plenty of taste and are better for you. Always choose meat that is fresh in appearance (red for beef, pink for pork), moist, and firm. It should not look gray. Store it in the refrigerator for no more than two days; if you don't plan to use fresh meat within two days, freeze it.

Beef and Pork

Come Back for More Chili

Some fans of chili like the dish on the *mild* side. Others like it *very* spicy. This recipe makes a batch of chili that is on the mild side. You can turn up the heat by adding some cayenne pepper.

Makes 4 servings

TOOLS

1 small bowl
Fork
Large sauté pan
Wooden spoon

INGREDIENTS

4 garlic cloves, minced
2 teaspoons ground cumin
1 teaspoon chili pepper
1/2 teaspoon salt and 1/4 teaspoon pepper
1 tablespoon extra virgin olive oil
1 pound extra lean ground beef
2 small onions, diced
1 small can (8 ounces) tomato sauce
1 cup low sodium beef broth
1 can (15–19 ounces) kidney beans, drained and rinsed
cayenne pepper (optional)

Come Back for More Chili

1. In a small bowl, combine the garlic, cumin, chili powder, salt, and pepper with a fork.

2. Add the olive oil to a large sauté pan and heat over medium-high for about 1 minute. Add the ground meat to the pan. Cook the meat, breaking it up with the edge of a wooden spoon. Stir occasionally until there is no more pink in the meat, about 8 to 10 minutes.

3. Reduce the heat to medium and add the diced onions to the meat. Use a clean wooden spoon to stir until the onions are softened, about 5 minutes.

4. Add the garlic mixture and stir for about 1 minute.

FUN FACT

What is the difference between chili and chile? Chili (with an "i" at the end) is the spicy dish that you eat from a bowl. Chile (with an "e" at the end) is the pepper pod that makes it spicy.

5. Add the tomato sauce, beef broth, and kidney beans. Stir until the mixture is combined and is bubbling briskly. Reduce the heat to simmer and allow the sauce to bubble gently. Cover the sauté pan with a lid.

6. Let the mixture simmer until the chili thickens and the flavors blend together, about 40 minutes. Stir occasionally to prevent sticking.

Serve your chili with small bowls of grated cheddar cheese and chopped onions to sprinkle on top. It is also great with cornbread.

7. Turn off the heat. Remove the lid, let the sauce rest for about 10 minutes, and then serve.

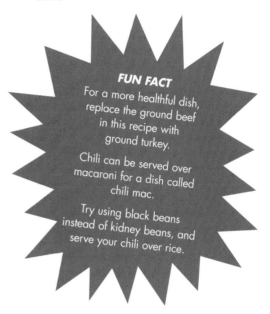

FUN FACT

For a more healthful dish, replace the ground beef in this recipe with ground turkey.

Chili can be served over macaroni for a dish called chili mac.

Try using black beans instead of kidney beans, and serve your chili over rice.

Nutrition Facts per Serving

Calories	360
Calories from fat	120
Total Fat	13 g
Saturated Fat	4 g
Monounsaturated Fat	7 g
Polyunsaturated Fat	1 g
Cholesterol	62 mg
Sodium	1061 mg
Total Carbohydrates	28 g
Dietary Fiber	6 g
Sugars	5 g
Protein	32 g

Melt in Your Mouth Meatloaf

Like a warm blanket on a cold night, meatloaf is all about comfort. This recipe is a down-home classic that is simple to make and a treat to eat.

Makes 4 to 6 servings

TOOLS

Small skillet
Wooden spoon
1 small bowl
Large stainless steel bowl
Whisk
9×5×3-inch loaf pan
Pastry brush

INGREDIENTS

1 tablespoon extra virgin olive oil
1 small onion, diced
2 eggs
1/2 cup plain dry bread crumbs
1 tablespoon garlic powder
1/2 tablespoon dried thyme leaves
1/4 tablespoon ground cayenne
2 tablespoons sweet relish
3/4 cup tomato sauce
1 1/2 pounds ground beef

1. Preheat oven to 350°F.

2. Add the oil to the skillet and heat over medium heat for about 1 minute. Place the onions in the skillet and stir until softened, about 5 minutes. Put them in a small bowl and set aside.

3. In a large stainless bowl, mix the eggs, bread crumbs, garlic powder, thyme, cayenne, relish, 1/2 cup of the tomato sauce, and the cooked onion. Stir with a whisk until the ingredients are combined.

4. Add the ground beef to the large bowl. Mix the ingredients with your hands to combine them.

5. Pack the mixture into a 9×5×3-inch loaf pan. Pat the meat mixture down smoothly.

Leftover meatloaf makes great sandwiches. Refrigerate it in one piece, and slice it after it gets cold. Meatloaf also freezes well. After it cools, wrap it in a double layer of aluminum foil and freeze. When you want to use it, thaw it in the refrigerator, and then heat it at 350°F for about 20 minutes.

6. Place 2 tablespoons of the remaining tomato sauce on top of the meatloaf. Using a pastry brush, brush the sauce evenly across the top.

7. Place the meatloaf in the oven and bake for 30 minutes.

8. Remove the pan from the oven and brush the remaining tomato sauce on top of the meatloaf. Place the pan back in the oven until the center of the top of the meatloaf is firm, about 25 to 30 minutes.

9. Let the meatloaf stand for about 10 minutes and then slice and serve.

✳ Always wash your hands thoroughly after touching raw meat.

Nutrition Facts per Serving	
Calories	354
Calories from fat	120
Total Fat	13g
Saturated Fat	3 g
Monounsaturated Fat	7 g
Polyunsaturated Fat	1 g
Cholesterol	183 mg
Sodium	537 mg
Total Carbohydrates	19 g
Dietary Fiber	2 g
Sugars	4 g
Protein	39 g

Best Beef Stew

The Best Beef Stew is the kind of recipe to make when you have plenty of time to cook. The delicious result is worth the wait. If you have any leftovers, they are even better the next day!

Makes 6 servings

TOOLS

1 small bowl
Dutch oven
Tongs
Wooden spoon with flat edge

INGREDIENTS

2 teaspoons salt and 1 teaspoon pepper
1 1/2 pounds beef stew meat in 1 1/2 to 2 inch chunks, patted dry

2 tablespoons extra virgin olive oil
2 medium onions, diced
4 large carrots, cut in half lengthwise, cut each half in 2-inch pieces
2 tablespoons tomato paste
2 1/2 cups low sodium beef broth
1 cup water
1/3 cup dry red lentils
4 large red-skinned potatoes, cut into 1 1/2-inch chunks

1. Preheat the oven to 325° F. In a small bowl, combine 1 1/2 teaspoons of the salt and the pepper. Pat the mixture into the beef.

2. Add the oil to the Dutch oven and heat over medium-high heat for about 1 minute. Add 1/3 of the meat to the pot, leaving some space around each piece.

3. Cook the meat using tongs to turn it until all sides are deep brown, about 8 minutes. Remove and place in a large bowl. Repeat step 2 with the remaining meat. Add oil to the pot as needed.

4. Reduce the heat to medium. Add the onions and the remaining salt to the pot. Cook until the onions are softened, about 5 minutes. As the onions cook, scrape the bottom of the pot with a wooden spoon.

5. Add the carrots and cook, stirring occasionally, for 3 minutes. Add the tomato paste and stir for 1 minute.

6. Add 1 cup of broth into the pot. Increase the heat to medium-high and cook, stirring continuously, until half of the liquid is gone, about 2 minutes.

7. Add the rest of the broth, water, potatoes, meat, and meat juices. Stir to combine and bring to a boil. Place a cover on the pot and place it in the oven.

8. Bake until the meat is tender, about 2 1/2 to 3 hours.

9. Remove from the oven and allow the stew to sit for about 10 minutes. Stir gently before serving.

Nutrition Facts per Serving	
Calories	684
Calories from fat	266
Total Fat	30 g
Saturated Fat	10 g
Monounsaturated Fat	14 g
Polyunsaturated Fat	2 g
Cholesterol	116 mg
Sodium	932 mg
Total Carbohydrates	57 g
Dietary Fiber	7 g
Sugars	8 g
Protein	42 g

Super Schnitzel

Schnitzel is a German word that means cutlet. It is a thin cutlet of meat that is breaded and fried in a little oil. This pork dish does not take long to make, and it is a great meal when paired with a crispy green salad.

Makes 4 servings

TOOLS

3 baking pans or pie plates
Fork
Paper towels
Large skillet
Tongs
Baking sheet
Meat mallet

INGREDIENTS

1/3 cup all-purpose flour
2 eggs
1 1/2 cups Italian style bread crumbs
4 boneless pork loin chops, pounded less
   than 1/4 inch thick
1/2 cup canola oil

1. Set the three baking pans in a row. Place flour in the first.

2. In the second pan, combine the eggs with 4 teaspoons of water. Beat the eggs lightly with a fork. Place bread crumbs in the third pan.

3. Pat the pounded pork loin chops dry with paper towels. Place one chop in the flour. Coat well on both sides and shake off the excess flour.

4. Place the chop in the egg mixture. Coat well on both sides and allow the excess egg to drip off.

5. Place the chop in the bread crumbs and press down. Shake off any excess bread crumbs. Place the chop on a large plate.

6. Repeat steps 3 to 5 with the remaining chops.

7. Add 1/2 cup of oil to cover the bottom of the skillet. Heat on medium-high heat for 1 minute.

8. Carefully place a breaded chop into the oil. Fry on the first side until golden brown, about 2 minutes. Use tongs to move the chop around in the oil.

9. Using the tongs, carefully turn the chop over. Fry on the second side for about 2 minutes until the chop is golden brown.

10. Place the chop on a baking sheet lined with paper towels to absorb any excess oil.

11. Repeat steps 8 to 10 with the remaining chops. Add more oil to the pan if needed. Serve the schnitzel with a mixed salad with citrus dressing.

Nutrition Facts per Serving	
Calories	591
Calories from fat	297
Total Fat	33 g
Saturated Fat	7 g
Monounsaturated Fat	16 g
Polyunsaturated Fat	6 g
Cholesterol	167 mg
Sodium	735 mg
Total Carbohydrates	38 g
Dietary Fiber	2 g
Sugars	2 g
Protein	33 g

If you notice that bread crumbs are piling up in the bottom of the skillet, it is time to change the oil. Pour out the used oil and wipe the pan with a paper towel to get rid of the loose bread crumbs. Add 1/2 cup of fresh oil and heat for about 30 seconds before continuing to prepare the schnitzel.

CHAPTER 10

Poultry and fish can be prepared and served in countless ways, from frying to baking to poaching, sautéing, and grilling. Here are some simple and easy favorites to get you started. After you've mastered some of the recipes here, you'll be ready to try many new and different chicken and fish dishes.

Paprika Mushroom Chicken

It's amazing what you can do with a can of soup! This recipe uses tomato soup to create a classic chicken dish. It is delicious served over rice or egg noodles.

Makes 4 servings

TOOLS

Large resealable plastic bag
2 large plates
Large sauté pan with lid
Tongs
Paring knife

INGREDIENTS

1/4 cup all-purpose flour
1 teaspoon seasoned salt
4 chicken breasts or legs, bone in
2 tablespoons extra virgin olive oil
3 medium onions, diced
1 teaspoon salt and 1/4 teaspoon pepper
1/2 pound brown mushrooms, sliced
1 can (10.75 ounces) condensed tomato
  soup, plus 1 can water
1 tablespoon paprika
2 bay leaves

Paprika Mushroom Chicken

1. Put the flour and seasoned salt in a large resealable plastic bag. Shake well. Add one or two of the chicken pieces to the flour mixture. Shake the bag to coat the chicken with the mixture.

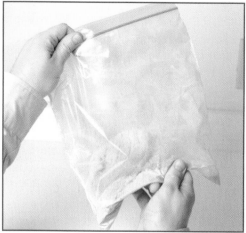

2. Remove the chicken from the bag. Shake off any excess flour, and place the chicken on a large plate.

3. Repeat steps 1 and 2 with the remaining pieces of chicken.

4. Add the oil to the sauté pan. Heat over medium-high heat for about 1 minute. Add two chicken pieces to the pan, with the skin side down.

5. Cook the chicken, turning once using tongs, until both sides are a deep golden brown. Remove the chicken and place it on a large, clean plate.

6. Repeat steps 4 and 5 with the remaining pieces of chicken. Add more oil to the pan if needed.

> You can change this dish to a creamy mushroom chicken by replacing the tomato soup with mushroom soup and leaving out the paprika.

7. Reduce the heat to medium. In the same pan add the onions and 1/2 teaspoon of salt. Stir often until softened, about 5 minutes.

8. Increase the heat to medium-high. Add the mushrooms and stir occasionally until lightly browned, about 5 minutes.

9. Add the tomato soup, water, paprika, remaining 1/2 teaspoon of salt, pepper, and bay leaves. Return the chicken to the pan. Coat the chicken with the sauce and bring to a boil.

10. Reduce the heat and simmer. Allow the mixture to gently bubble. Cover the sauté pan with a lid.

11. Let the mixture simmer, stirring occasionally, until the chicken is tender and the juices run clear when the chicken is pierced with a paring knife, about 40 minutes.

12. Turn off the heat. Remove the lid and let the pan sit for about 10 minutes. Remove the bay leaves and serve the chicken.

FUN FACT

The peppers that are used to make paprika have approximately 9 times the vitamin C as tomatoes of similar weight. The word paprika is from a Middle European word that means "the one that is hot."

Nutrition Facts per Serving	
Calories	319
Calories from fat	79
Total Fat	9 g
Saturated Fat	1 g
Monounsaturated Fat	6 g
Polyunsaturated Fat	1 g
Cholesterol	68 mg
Sodium	1465 mg
Total Carbohydrates	28 g
Dietary Fiber	3 g
Sugars	11 g
Protein	31 g

Asian Chicken Stir-Fry

This delectable chicken dish includes a lot of vegetables, but there is always room for more. Add in carrots or bean sprouts or any of your favorites to make it your own signature dish.

Makes 4 servings

TOOLS

1 small bowl
Whisk
Large sauté pan
2 wooden spoons
Large bowl

INGREDIENTS

1/2 cup oyster sauce
2 tablespoons soy sauce
2 garlic cloves, minced
3 tablespoons extra virgin olive oil
1 pound chicken stir-fry strips
1 medium onion, cut into 1/2-inch slices
1/2 pound fresh snow peas, strings removed
1 medium zucchini, cut into sticks
1 red pepper, cut into strips
1 can (14 ounces) baby corn, drained and rinsed

1. In a small bowl, combine the oyster sauce, soy sauce, and garlic using a whisk.

2. Add two tablespoons of the oil to a large sauté pan and heat over medium-high heat for about 1 minute. Add the chicken strips to the pan and cook. Toss the chicken with two wooden spoons as it cooks until it is no longer pink, about 4 minutes. Place in a bowl and set aside.

3. Add the remaining oil to the pan. Add the onion and snow peas. Toss the vegetables with the wooden spoons until they are cooked. Add the zucchini and red pepper to the pan and continue to toss.

5. Add the baby corn, chicken and oyster sauce mixture to the pan, stirring continuously for about 1 minute to combine the sauce and all the ingredients.

4. Serve the dish over rice or Asian noodles.

You can use shrimp or scallops instead of chicken in this recipe. Substitute 1 pound of raw shrimp or scallops for the chicken in step 2 and cook for 2 minutes. Put in a bowl and set aside. Add the shrimp or scallops back to the pan in step 4.

FUN FACT
Peas are one of the earliest known cultivated plants. They have even been found in Egyptian tombs.

Nutrition Facts per Serving

Calories	385
Calories from fat	122
Total Fat	14g
Saturated Fat	2 g
Monounsaturated Fat	9 g
Polyunsaturated Fat	2 g
Cholesterol	66 mg
Sodium	866 mg
Total Carbohydrates	37 g
Dietary Fiber	6 g
Sugars	9 g
Protein	33 g

Pesto Chicken Roll-Ups

The flavors of pesto and mozzarella cheese make these pretty roll-ups a great party food that everyone will enjoy. The rolls can be prepared a day ahead, covered in plastic wrap and kept in the refrigerator until you are ready to bake them.

Makes 4 servings

TOOLS

Baking sheet
Parchment paper
1 small bowl
1 large plate
Pastry brush
16 heavy toothpicks
Meat mallet
Chef's knife

INGREDIENTS

1 teaspoon salt and 1/4 teaspoon pepper
4 boneless chicken breasts, pounded 1/4-inch thick
4 tablespoons basil pesto
1/2 cup shredded mozzarella cheese
4 teaspoons extra virgin olive oil
2 tablespoons Dijon mustard
4 tablespoons dry bread crumbs

1. Preheat the oven to 375°F.

2. Cover the bottom of a baking sheet with parchment paper.

3. In a small bowl, combine the salt and pepper. Pat the mixture into both sides of the chicken. On a large plate, place one chicken breast, smooth side down, with the narrowest end closest to you.

4. Put 1 tablespoon of pesto onto the center of the breast. Spread the pesto evenly over the chicken using a pastry brush. Sprinkle 2 tablespoons of shredded cheese over the pesto. Keep a 1/2 inch cheese-free border around the edge of the breast.

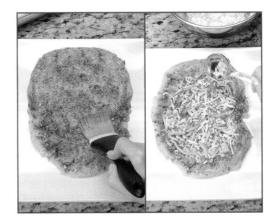

5. Start at the end of the chicken closest to you. Carefully roll up the breast. Push 4 toothpicks into the breast, securing the loose end so that it does not unroll. Place the breast, toothpick side down, on the pre-pared baking sheet.

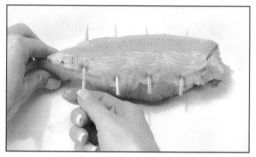

6. Repeat steps 3 to 5 with the remaining chicken breasts. Wash the pastry brush in hot, soapy water when you are done.

7. Slowly pour 1 teaspoon of oil over each breast. Use the clean pastry brush to coat the top and sides of each breast. Wash the pastry brush in hot, soapy water when you are done.

8. Put 1 1/2 teaspoons of Dijon mustard on top of each breast. Use the clean pastry brush to coat the top and sides of each breast.

9. Carefully sprinkle 1 tablespoon of bread crumbs over the top and along the sides of each breast. Use your fingers to pat the crumbs onto the sides.

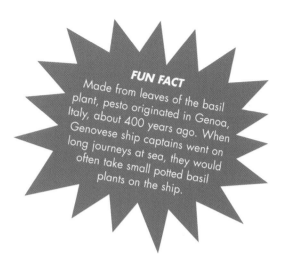

FUN FACT

Made from leaves of the basil plant, pesto originated in Genoa, Italy, about 400 years ago. When Genovese ship captains went on long journeys at sea, they would often take small potted basil plants on the ship.

10. Bake until the chicken is firm and no longer pink inside, about 20 to 25 minutes.

11. Remove the chicken from the oven and let it stand for 5 minutes before remov-ing the toothpicks.

12. Using a chef's knife, slice each breast 1/2-inch to 1-inch thick before serving.

Nutrition Facts per Serving	
Calories	272
Calories from fat	114
Total Fat	13 g
Saturated Fat	4g
Monounsaturated Fat	6 g
Polyunsaturated Fat	2 g
Cholesterol	81 mg
Sodium	952 mg
Total Carbohydrates	6 g
Dietary Fiber	1 g
Sugars	1 g
Protein	32 g

Shrimp Scampi

If you are a fan of seafood, shrimp scampi is
a great dish for you. In a sauce of butter and
garlic, these shrimp are perfect when served
on a bed of rice or a nest of yummy linguini.

Makes 4 servings

TOOLS

1 medium bowl
Whisk
Medium-sized fine mesh strainer
Large skillet
Wooden spoon

INGREDIENTS

1/4 cup all-purpose flour
1/4 teaspoon salt and 1/4 teaspoon pepper
1 pound large raw shrimp, peeled, cleaned,
  and patted dry
2 tablespoons extra virgin olive oil
1 shallot, minced
1/2 cup bottled clam juice
1 tablespoon fresh lemon juice
1/4 cup unsalted butter (1/2 stick, cut in
  cubes)
2 tablespoons finely chopped Italian parsley

1. In a medium bowl, mix together the flour,
   salt, and pepper with a whisk. Add the
   shrimp to the bowl. Mix well with your
   hands to coat the shrimp with the flour
   mixture.

2. Place the floured shrimp in a medium-sized fine mesh strainer held over the sink. Shake the strainer to remove any excess flour from the shrimp. Set aside.

3. Add the oil to the skillet and heat for about 1 minute over medium heat. Add the shrimp, minced shallot, and garlic. Cook, stirring continuously, for 1 minute.

You can substitute baby spinach for parsley in this recipe. Wash and spin dry about a cup of baby spinach leaves and add them to the sauté pan in step 4.

FUN FACT

In 2006, a man fishing off the coast of Colombia, South America, caught what may be the world's largest known shrimp. It was a tiger shrimp that was 16 inches long.

4. Add the clam juice, lemon juice, and butter to the skillet.

5. Cook, stirring occasionally, until the shrimp are just firm and pink and the sauce has thickened slightly, about 3 minutes.

6. Turn off the heat and stir the chopped parsley into the mixture. Serve with pasta or rice.

Nutrition Facts per Serving

Calories	315
Calories from fat	178
Total Fat	20 g
Saturated Fat	8 g
Monounsaturated Fat	8 g
Polyunsaturated Fat	2 g
Cholesterol	203 mg
Sodium	382 mg
Total Carbohydrates	8 g
Dietary Fiber	0 g
Sugars	0 g
Protein	24 g

Pan-Fried Tilapia

Tilapia is a popular fish. You'll find it on many restaurant menus. Follow this recipe to make fillets that can be served for dinner, lunch, a light supper, or on a crusty roll as a terrific sandwich.

Makes 4 servings

TOOLS

Pie pan
Whisk
1 large skillet
Spatula
Platter
Aluminum foil
1 large plate

INGREDIENTS

2 tablespoons all-purpose flour
1/2 teaspoon garlic powder
1/4 teaspoon dry mustard
1/4 teaspoon curry powder
1/2 teaspoon salt and 1/8 teaspoon pepper
4 tilapia fillets, washed and patted dry
1/4 cup extra virgin olive oil

1. In a shallow pan, mix together the flour, garlic powder, dry mustard, curry powder, salt, and pepper with a whisk.

2. Place one fillet in the flour mixture and coat well on both sides. Shake off any excess flour mixture and place the fillet on a large plate.

3. Repeat step 2 with the remaining fillets.

4. Add the oil to the skillet and heat over medium-high heat for about 1 minute. Carefully place two fillets in the skillet.

5. Cook the fillets. Use a spatula to turn once so that they are golden brown on each side and the flesh is firm, about 4 minutes.

6. Place the fillets on a platter and cover loosely with aluminum foil.

7. Repeat steps 2 to 6 with the two remaining fillets. Serve immediately.

Tilapia fillets are great with homemade tartar sauce. Make the sauce by combining 1/3 cup low-fat mayonnaise, 1 1/2 tablespoons sweet relish, 1 tablespoon minced onion, 1 1/2 teaspoons fresh lemon juice, 1/8 teaspoon salt, and a pinch of pepper. Stir well and serve with piping hot fish fillets.

Nutrition Facts per Serving

Calories	361
Calories from fat	153
Total Fat	17 g
Saturated Fat	3 g
Monounsaturated Fat	11 g
Polyunsaturated Fat	2g
Cholesterol	81 mg
Sodium	441 mg
Total Carbohydrates	3 g
Dietary Fiber	0 g
Sugars	0 g
Protein	45 g

Coconut Curry Chowder

The flavors of coconut and curry make this Southeast Asian dish a real treat that is quick and easy to prepare. If you prefer, you can substitute chicken for the halibut.

Makes 4 servings

TOOLS

Large sauté pan
2 wooden spoons

INGREDIENTS

1 1/2 pounds halibut fillets, skin removed
1 tablespoon extra virgin olive oil
2 shallots, halved and thinly sliced
2 garlic cloves, thinly sliced
1 can (14 ounces) light coconut milk
1/2 cup low sodium chicken broth
1 tablespoon honey
1 teaspoon Thai curry paste
3/4 cup frozen peas (do not thaw)

1. Rinse the halibut fillets under cold running water. Cut into 1-inch cubes and set aside.

2. Add the oil to the pan and heat over medium heat for about 1 minute. Add the shallots to the pan and cook, stirring often, for 2 minutes.

3. Add the garlic to the pan and cook, stirring often, for 1 minute.

4. Add the coconut milk, chicken broth, honey, and curry paste to the pan. Stir to combine.

5. Bring the mixture to a simmer so that it is bubbling gently. Cook, stirring often, for about 5 minutes.

6. Add the frozen peas and bring the mixture back to a simmer. Add the cubes of fish and stir.

7. Increase the heat to medium high and bring back to a simmer. Toss gently using two wooden spoons.

8. Cook until the fish is firm, about 5 minutes. Adjust the heat so that the chowder continues to simmer for 5 minutes. Serve hot.

Tip ● Tip ● Tip ● Tip ●

To make a complete meal, serve a bowl of this chowder with a side of jasmine rice and a salad with Asian dressing.

Tip ● Tip ● Tip ● T

Nutrition Facts per Serving	
Calories	324
Calories from fat	98
Total Fat	11 g
Saturated Fat	6 g
Monounsaturated Fat	3 g
Polyunsaturated Fat	1 g
Cholesterol	97 mg
Sodium	954 mg
Total Carbohydrates	14 g
Dietary Fiber	2 g
Sugars	8 g
Protein	35 g

CHAPTER 11

It's economical and healthy, as well as tasty, to create a meal using only vegetables. You don't always have to have meat for dinner! Here are some recipes to introduce you to vegetarian cooking.

Very Vegetarian

Hearty Chickpea Curry

If you are cooking for a group, this dish will please everyone. Your vegetarian (and non-vegetarian) friends will thank you for it.

Makes 4 servings

TOOLS

Small bowl
Large saucepan
Wooden spoon
Serving bowls

INGREDIENTS

2 garlic cloves, minced
1 tablespoon curry powder or paste
1 teaspoon ground cumin
2 tablespoons extra virgin olive oil
2 medium onions, diced into 1/4-inch pieces
1 can (28 ounces) diced tomatoes
2 cans (15 to 19 ounces each) chickpeas, drained and rinsed
3 medium carrots, sliced 1/8-inch thick
1 teaspoon salt and 1/4 teaspoon pepper
1 large green pepper, diced into 1/2-inch pieces

Hearty Chickpea Curry

1. In a small bowl, combine the garlic, curry powder (or paste), and cumin. Set aside.

2. Add the oil to a large saucepan or sauté pan over medium heat until hot, about 1 to 2 minutes.

3. Place the onions in the pan and stir often until softened, about 5 minutes.

4. Add the garlic and curry mixture to the onions. Stir continuously for 1 minute.

5. Add the tomatoes, chickpeas, carrots, salt, and pepper to the mixture. Stir until combined. Increase the heat to high and bring the mixture to a boil.

6. Once the mixture is boiling, reduce the heat and simmer until it is gently bubbling. Cover the pan with a lid.

7. Let the mixture simmer, stirring occasionally, until the carrots are slightly firm but can be pierced with a fork, about 20 minutes.

8. Remove the cover, stir in the green pepper, and continue to cook uncovered until the green pepper can be pierced with a fork, about 5 minutes.

9. Remove the pan from the heat and serve.

Tip

To add extra flavor, chop and sprinkle fresh cilantro over your chickpea curry. Serve this dish with rice and a side salad. If you want a creamier texture, add a small can of coconut milk to your curry during step 8.

FUN FACT
There are approximately 80 important spices regularly used in cooking. Because of its climate, 50 of those spices grow well in India. Curry powder is a blend of spices that usually includes coriander, turmeric, cumin, and fenugreek.

Nutrition Facts per Serving	
Calories	504
Calories from fat	118
Total Fat	13 g
Saturated Fat	2 g
Monounsaturated Fat	7 g
Polyunsaturated Fat	3 g
Cholesterol	0 mg
Sodium	1676 mg
Total Carbohydrates	80 g
Dietary Fiber	20 g
Sugars	21 g
Protein	22 g

Pan-Roasted Vegetables with Bulgur

Ready to try something new? Bulgur is a form of cracked wheat. It is a tasty, chewy grain that is a perfect match for garden vegetables.

Makes 4 servings

TOOLS

Large bowl
Clean plate
Fine mesh strainer
Spoon
Large sauté pan
2 wooden spoons
Medium bowl

INGREDIENTS

1 cup bulgur

1 teaspoon salt

1 serving Fat-Free Tomato Dressing (see page 85)

3 tablespoons extra virgin olive oil

1 medium onion, halved and cut into 1/2-inch slices

1 large red pepper and 1 large yellow pepper cut into 1-inch chunks

2 zucchinis, halved lengthwise and cut into 3/4-inch chunks

2 tablespoons balsamic vinegar

1 can (15 to 19 ounces) bean medley, drained and rinsed

1. Place the bulgur, salt, and 3 cups of water in a large bowl and stir. Cover the bowl with a large plate and set aside until the bulgur is almost soft, about 10 to 15 minutes.

2. Drain the bulgur into a fine mesh strainer. Press gently with the back of a spoon to remove the excess water. Place the bulgur back into the bowl and stir with a fork.

3. Pour the dressing over the bulgur and stir well. Set aside.

4. Add 2 tablespoons of oil to a large sauté pan over medium-high heat for 1 or 2 minutes. Carefully swirl the pan to coat the surface with the oil.

5. Add the onions and the peppers to the pan in a single layer. Cook without stirring for 2 minutes. Using two wooden spoons, toss the vegetables and cook for 2 minutes.

6. Place the onions and peppers in a medium bowl and set aside.

7. Add 1 tablespoon of oil to the pan. Repeat steps 5 and 6 with the zucchini. Add the zucchini to the medium bowl with the other vegetables.

8. Add the vinegar to the medium bowl and toss with a serving spoon to coat all of the vegetables.

9. Add the beans to the large bowl of bulgur and combine using the serving spoon.

10. Serve the pan-roasted vegetables over the bulgur and bean mixture.

Nutrition Facts per Serving	
Calories	381
Calories from fat	110
Total Fat	12 g
Saturated Fat	2 g
Monounsaturated Fat	8 g
Polyunsaturated Fat	2 g
Cholesterol	0 mg
Sodium	1086 mg
Total Carbohydrates	58 g
Dietary Fiber	15 g
Sugars	11 g
Protein	13 g

CHAPTER 12

Everyone loves dessert. On the following pages are a few classics and some brand new creations that are easy to make and delicious. You'll be everybody's favorite cook when you serve up these goodies.

Anytime Muffins

Tangy cranberries and sweet orange juice make these muffins a great way to start the day or a tasty evening snack.

Makes 12 muffins

TOOLS

1 muffin pan
Whisk
1 large mixing bowl
1 medium mixing bowl
Rubber spatula
1/3 cup measuring cup
Cooling rack

INGREDIENTS

2 cups all-purpose flour
1 cup packed brown sugar
1 1/2 teaspoons baking soda
1/2 teaspoon salt
3/4 cup quick oats (not instant)
2 eggs
3/4 cup orange juice
3/4 cup 1% milk
1/2 cup vegetable oil
1 cup frozen unsweetened cranberries (do not thaw)

Anytime Muffins

1. Preheat oven to 375°F.

2. Lightly coat the cups of a muffin pan with vegetable oil or baking spray. You can also use paper muffin cups if you like.

3. In a large mixing bowl, add the flour, brown sugar, baking soda, and salt. Mix well with a whisk.

4. Add the oats to the mixture. With the whisk, stir until all of the ingredients are combined, and then set aside.

5. In a medium mixing bowl, add the eggs, orange juice, milk, and oil. Stir with a whisk until all the ingredients are combined. Set aside.

6. Add the frozen cranberries to the flour and oat mixture. Then pour the liquid mixture into the large bowl.

7. Using a rubber spatula, stir the batter to combine. Do not overmix.

8. Use a 1/3 cup measuring cup to scoop the batter into the muffin cups. Fill each one completely.

9. Bake until the tops of the muffins are firm to the touch, about 20 to 24 minutes.

10. Remove the pan from the oven and let the muffins cool for about 5 minutes. Lift the muffins out of the pan and place them on a cooling rack.

FUN FACT
Fresh ripe cranberries bounce. They float, too. At harvest time, producers often flood the marshes where the berries grow. Ripe cranberries float to the surface.

You can freeze Anytime Muffins by wrapping them individually in plastic wrap and storing them in a resealable freezer bag. When you want to enjoy a warm muffin, simply take one from the freezer, unwrap it, and pop it in the microwave for about 1 minute.

Nutrition Facts per Serving

Calories	276
Calories from fat	100
Total Fat	11 g
Saturated Fat	2 g
Monounsaturated Fat	7 g
Polyunsaturated Fat	1 g
Cholesterol	32 mg
Sodium	280 mg
Total Carbohydrates	40 g
Dietary Fiber	1 g
Sugars	21 g
Protein	4 g

Ultimate Chocolate Chip Cookies

Nothing could be better than warm, chewy cookies straight from the oven! You can make yours with milk chocolate chips, white chocolate, or even creamy butterscotch chips.

Makes approximately 48 cookies

TOOLS

2 non-stick baking sheets
Parchment paper (optional)
Whisk
Rubber spatula
Teaspoon
1 small bowl
1 small microwave-safe bowl
1 medium mixing bowl
1 large mixing bowl
Electric hand mixer

INGREDIENTS

2 1/4 cups all-purpose flour
1 teaspoon baking soda
1/2 teaspoon salt
2 eggs
1 cup unsalted butter, cut in 1/2-inch slices
3/4 cup granulated sugar
2/3 cup packed brown sugar
2 teaspoons vanilla extract
2 cups chocolate chips

1. Preheat the oven to 375°F.

2. Use two non-stick baking sheets, or cover the bottom of two baking sheets with parchment paper.

3. In a medium bowl, mix the flour, baking soda, and salt with a whisk. Set aside.

4. Break the eggs into a small bowl and set aside.

5. In a small microwave-safe bowl, melt the butter in the microwave for 30 seconds. Stir. Melt 30 seconds more.

6. Pour the melted butter into a large bowl. Add the granulated sugar, brown sugar, and vanilla to the bowl.

7. Using an electric hand mixer, beat the ingredients together at medium speed for about 2 minutes.

8. Add the eggs to the sugar mixture and beat at medium speed until the ingredients are combined.

9. Add in one quarter of the flour mixture, beating at low speed until thoroughly combined.

10. Repeat step 9 for each of the three remaining quarters of the flour mixture. Use a rubber spatula to scrape any dough from the beaters into the bowl. Use the spatula to stir the chocolate chips into the dough.

11. Drop one heaping teaspoonful of dough at a time onto the baking sheets. Leave about 1 1/2 inches between each cookie.

12. Bake each sheet separately on the center rack of the oven. Bake until the cookie tops are golden brown and the edges are lightly browned, about 9 to 12 minutes.

13. Remove the baking sheet and place it on a heat-safe surface. Let the cookies cool for about three minutes.

14. Using a spatula, place the cookies on a large tray or cooling rack to cool completely.

Nutrition Facts per Serving	
Calories	132
Calories from fat	60
Total Fat	7 g
Saturated Fat	4 g
Monounsaturated Fat	1 g
Polyunsaturated Fat	0 g
Cholesterol	18 mg
Sodium	5 mg
Total Carbohydrates	17 g
Dietary Fiber	0 g
Sugars	12 g
Protein	1 g

Double Chocolate Brownies

These brownies are so rich and gooey that they don't need any frosting. Top them with a dollop of whipped cream and sliced strawberries if you like. They are also delicious served plain with a cold glass of milk.

Makes 16 servings

TOOLS

8×8-inch baking pan
Medium saucepan
Heat-proof spatula
1 medium mixing bowl
Whisk
Small bowl
Toothpick

INGREDIENTS

4 ounces unsweetened chocolate (4 squares),
  cut in quarters
1/2 cup semi-sweet chocolate chips
1/2 cup unsalted butter, cut into small chunks
3 eggs
3/4 cup granulated sugar
2 teaspoons vanilla extract
1/2 cup all-purpose flour
1/2 teaspoon baking powder
1/4 teaspoon salt

1. Preheat the oven to 350°F.

2. Lightly coat an 8×8-inch baking pan with butter.

3. Fill a medium saucepan with 1 inch of water. Place the saucepan on the stove and bring to a simmer so that the water is gently bubbling.

4. Place the unsweetened chocolate, chocolate chips, and butter in a medium glass or stainless steel bowl. Place the bowl over the saucepan, making sure that the bottom of the bowl does not touch the water.

5. The bowl will get hot, so use an oven mitt to hold it as you occasionally stir the ingredients with a heat-proof spatula. Stir for 5 minutes or until all of the ingredients are melted.

6. Remove the bowl from the saucepan and set aside on a heat-proof surface.

7. Place the eggs and sugar in a medium mixing bowl. Whisk for about 2 to 3 minutes until the mixture is light and fluffy. Whisk in the vanilla until blended.

8. Slowly whisk the cooled chocolate mixture into the egg mixture until they are completely blended.

9. In a small bowl, whisk together the flour, baking powder, and salt. Add the mixture to the chocolate and egg mixture. Blend well using a rubber spatula. Pour the batter into the prepared baking pan. Use the spatula to spread the batter evenly.

10. Bake until a toothpick poked into the center of the pan comes out with just a trace of moist chocolate on it, about 20 to 25 minutes.

11. Remove the baking pan from the oven and allow to cool completely in the pan before cutting into squares.

If you like your brownies a little nutty, fold in a cup of chopped pecans or walnuts just before you pour the batter into the baking pan.

Nutrition Facts per Serving

Calories	188
Calories from fat	113
Total Fat	13 g
Saturated Fat	8 g
Monounsaturated Fat	4 g
Polyunsaturated Fat	1 g
Cholesterol	50 mg
Sodium	52 mg
Total Carbohydrates	20 g
Dietary Fiber	2 g
Sugars	14 g
Protein	3 g

Dreamy Cheesecake

Cheesecake is the best thing that ever happened to cream cheese. Cut into squares, this tasty treat is great on its own, or topped with berries or chocolate sauce.

Makes 24 squares

TOOLS

1 9×13-inch baking pan
1 small bowl
1 medium mixing bowl
Fork
1 large mixing bowl
Electric hand mixer
Rubber spatula
Cooling rack

INGREDIENTS

3 eggs
1 1/2 cups graham cracker crumbs
3/4 cup granulated sugar
1/2 cup melted unsalted butter
1 pound reduced fat cream cheese, softened
1 cup part-skim ricotta cheese
1 cup low-fat sour cream
1/4 teaspoon salt
1 tablespoon fresh lemon juice
2 tablespoons vanilla extract

1. Preheat the oven to 350°F.

2. Lightly coat the bottom and sides of a 9×13-inch baking pan with vegetable shortening or baking spray.

3. Break the eggs into a small bowl and set aside.

4. In a medium mixing bowl, combine the graham cracker crumbs, 2 tablespoons of sugar, and the melted butter. Stir with a fork to blend well.

FUN FACT
A form of cheesecake was one of the foods served to the athletes at the first Olympic Games held in 776 B.C. in ancient Greece.

5. Use your fingers to spread the graham cracker mixture evenly over the bottom of the prepared baking pan. Pat the crumb mixture down firmly.

6. Place the cream cheese and remaining sugar in a large mixing bowl. Use a hand mixer at low speed to beat the cheese and sugar until it is smooth. Add the eggs, ricotta cheese, sour cream, salt, lemon juice, and vanilla to the bowl. Beat the ingredients at low speed until they are creamy.

If over-baked, cheesecake can crack. Watch your bake time carefully. Once your cheesecake has completely cooled after baking, place plastic wrap directly onto the top to prevent it from drying until you are ready to serve it.

7. Pour the cream cheese mixture evenly over the graham cracker crust in the pan. Use a rubber spatula to remove all of the batter from the bowl and spread it evenly in the pan.

8. Bake about 22 to 27 minutes. A 3-inch square at the center of the cheesecake should still look slightly liquid when you jiggle the pan. The rest of the cheesecake should be firm. It will look like it is a little under-baked.

9. Place the pan on a cooling rack for 15 minutes. Then put it in the refrigerator for at least 2 hours before serving. Cut into squares and serve.

Nutrition Facts per Serving	
Calories	161
Calories from fat	91
Total Fat	10 g
Saturated Fat	6 g
Monounsaturated Fat	3 g
Polyunsaturated Fat	1 g
Cholesterol	51 mg
Sodium	137 mg
Total Carbohydrates	13 g
Dietary Fiber	0 g
Sugars	8 g
Protein	5 g

Lemony Pound Cake

This lemony pound cake is moist and buttery and just right for lemon lovers.

Makes 10 servings

TOOLS

1 9×5×3-inch loaf pan
Medium-sized fine mesh strainer
1 medium mixing bowl
Whisk
Stand mixer (or hand mixer)
Rubber spatula
Toothpick

INGREDIENTS

1 2/3 cups cake flour
1 teaspoon baking powder
1/2 teaspoon salt
1 tablespoon finely grated lemon zest
4 eggs
1 cup unsalted butter (softened)
1 1/4 cups granulated sugar
1/4 cup fresh lemon juice
2 teaspoons vanilla extract

1. Preheat oven to 325°F.

2. Spray the sides of a 9×5×3-inch loaf pan with baking spray.

3. Place a medium-sized fine mesh strainer over a medium mixing bowl. Use the strainer to sift the flour, baking powder, and salt into the bowl. Shake the strainer or stir with a spoon to force the ingredients through the mesh.

4. Add the lemon zest to the bowl and stir with a whisk.

5. In a small mixing bowl, gently beat the eggs with a whisk and set aside.

6. Use a stand mixer or a hand mixer to beat the butter at medium speed until it is creamy and light in color, about 3 minutes. Continue to beat the butter and slowly add the sugar until the mixture is light and fluffy, about 5 to 6 minutes.

7. Continue to beat as you add one third of the beaten eggs. Combine for about 30 seconds.

8. Repeat step 7 for each of the two thirds of the remaining eggs. Beat until the mixture is airy, about 2 minutes.

9. Add half of the flour mixture and blend well with a rubber spatula.

10. Add the lemon juice and blend well. Blend in the remaining flour mixture, and then blend in the vanilla.

11. Using the rubber spatula, spread the batter evenly in the prepared loaf pan and smooth the top.

12. Bake until the cake is a deep golden brown and a toothpick in the center comes out clean, about 60 to 70 minutes.

13. Remove the cake from the oven and place the pan on a cooling rack for 15 minutes. Remove the cake from the pan and allow it to cool completely before slicing.

Don't take shortcuts when you beat the cake batter. Beating butter and sugar together is called *creaming*. It's how you get air bubbles into the butter. The bubbles guarantee a soft fluffy cake.

Nutrition Facts per Serving

Calories	371
Calories from fat	178
Total Fat	20 g
Saturated Fat	12 g
Monounsaturated Fat	5 g
Polyunsaturated Fat	1 g
Cholesterol	123 mg
Sodium	193 mg
Total Carbohydrates	44 g
Dietary Fiber	0 g
Sugars	25 g
Protein	4 g

Glossary

A

Al dente
An Italian phrase that means "to the tooth." It is used to describe pasta that is slightly firm, but soft enough not to stick to your teeth.

B

Baste
Spoon or brush any liquid over food while it is cooking. Basting keeps the food moist and adds flavor.

Batter
An uncooked fluid mixture that usually contains flour. A batter is usually made for cakes and other baked goods.

Beat
Mix ingredients quickly until they are blended. Beating adds air to ingredients such as eggs or cream.

Blanch
Dunk vegetables or fruit in boiling water for a few seconds to loosen the skin or improve the color or flavor.

Bread
Coat foods to be sautéed or fried with a bread crumb or flour mixture.

Broil
Cook food below a heat source, such as a broiler in an oven.

C

Chiffonade
Roll and cut herbs or leafy vegetables to create strips.

Chop
Cut food in small irregular pieces.

Cube
Cut food into square pieces 1/2 inch or larger.

D

Dice
Cut food into cubed or square pieces, about 1/4 inch to 3/4 inch in size.

Dough
A flour mixture that is thick enough to spoon or roll for foods such as cookies, pie crusts, and bread.

F

Fold
Gently combine a light airy ingredient, such as beaten egg whites, into a heavier mixture, such as a cake batter.

Fry
Cook foods in hot oil in a pan on the stove.

G

Grate
Rub food, such as cheese or vegetables, across the sharp holes of a grater. Grating is also called shredding.

Grease
Coat the surface of a pan with oil or butter.

J

Julienne
Cut food into very thin strips.

K

Knead
Folding and pressing dough with a turning motion until the dough is smooth and elastic.

M

Marinate
Soak meat, poultry, fish, or vegetables in a seasoned, liquid mixture to add flavor before cooking.

Mince
Cut food into very fine pieces.

P

Pesto
A sauce made of crushed basil leaves, garlic, pine nuts, and olive oil.

Pureé
Blend food until it is smooth and mixed thoroughly.

S

Sauté
Cook food in a small amount of oil in a pan on the stove.

Sear
Brown the surface of meat, poultry, or fish by cooking briefly over very high heat.

Simmer
Cook liquids on the stove at a temperature just below the boiling point.

Steam
Cook food in a metal basket that is over but not in boiling water so that the steam cooks the food.

Z

Zest
To remove thin strips of the colored outer skin of citrus fruit, such as lemons or oranges.

Metric Conversion Chart

VOLUME

U.S. Units	Metric
1/4 teaspoon	1 ml
1/2 teaspoon	2 ml
1 teaspoon	5 ml
1 tablespoon	15 ml
1/4 cup	50 ml
1/3 cup	75 ml
1/2 cup	125 ml
2/3 cup	150 ml
3/4 cup	175 ml
1 cup	250 ml
1 quart	1 liter
1 1/2 quarts	1.5 liters
2 quarts	2 liters
2 1/2 quarts	2.5 liters
3 quarts	3 liters
4 quarts	4 liters

TEMPERATURES

Fahrenheit	Celsius
32°	0°
212°	100°
250°	120°
275°	140°
300°	150°
325°	160°
350°	180°
375°	190°
400°	200°
425°	220°
450°	230°
475°	240°
500°	260°

WEIGHT

U.S. Units	Metric
1 ounce	30 grams
2 ounces	55 grams
3 ounces	85 grams
4 ounces (1/4 pound)	115 grams
8 ounces (1/2 pound)	225 grams
16 ounces (1 pound)	455 grams

MEASUREMENTS

Inches	Centimeters
1/8	0.3 (3 millimeters)
1/4	0.6 (6 millimeters)
1/2	1.3
3/4	1.9
1	2.5
1 1/2	3.8
2	5

INDEX

V

vanilla, 21
vegetable pastas, 25
vegetable peelers, 4
    tomatoes, peeling, 44–45
vegetables. *See also* specific types
    cleaning, 29
    cooking times for, 64–65
    in From the Garden Soup, 80–81
    Omelet, Veggie Cheese, 109–111
    Pan-Roasted Vegetables with Bulgur, 148–149
    pinwheels with, 79
    Roasted Vegetables, 100–101
    selecting, 29
    storing, 29
Veggie Cheese Omelet, 109–111
vinegars. *See also* balsamic vinegar
    Asian Style Dressing, rice vinegar in, 87
    Confetti Potato Salad, sherry vinegar in, 92–93
vitamins
    in eggs, 27
    in paprika, 133

W

walnuts
    in Brownies, Double Chocolate, 157
    in Summery Spinach Salad, 89
washing. *See* cleaning
watercress, 31
whipping techniques, 40–41

whiskey in Irish stew, 68
whisks, 5
    whipping by hand with, 40
white potatoes, 26
white rice, 23
whole wheat pastas, 25
wild rice, 23
winter squash
    Buttery Butternut Soup, 82–83
    cooking times and methods for, 65
woks, 67
wooden spoons, 7
Worcestershire sauce in Caesar Salad, Classic, 90–91

Y

yellow pepper in Pan-Roasted Vegetables with Bulgur, 148–149
yellow potatoes, 26
yogurt
    in Indian Dressing, 87
    in Summery Spinach Salad, 88–89
Yukon Gold potatoes, 26
    Mashed Potatoes, 98–99

Z

zesting citrus, 51
zucchini
    in Asian Chicken Stir-Fry, 134–135
    in Pan-Roasted Vegetables with Bulgur, 148–149

ABOUT THE AUTHOR

maranGraphics Inc. is a family-run business based in Ontario, Canada.

For over 30 years, the Maran family has produced
friendly and easy-to-use visual learning books.